GET IT TOGETHER

GET IT TOGETHER

Brian Cranwell

National Extension College

ISBN 0 86082 763 1

© National Extension College Trust Ltd 1986

National Extension College
18 Brooklands Avenue
Cambridge CB2 2HN

The National Extension College is an adult teaching
body providing education through correspondence
courses, publishing, tapes, computer software, slides
and kits. As a non-profit-distributing company,
registered as a charity, all monies received by NEC are
used to extend and improve the range of services
provided.

Designed by Jim Reader
Cover designed by Vicky Squires
Cartoons by Brian Warwick and (p. 158) Chris Meade

Production Services by Book Production Consultants,
Cambridge

Typeset by Cambridge Photosetting Services

Contents

ABOUT THE AUTHOR

Brian Cranwell became involved in unemployment issues whilst working in Central and East Africa in the post-independence 1960s, little realising that he would find the same issues escalating in the United Kingdom when he returned in the 1970s. He soon became involved in youth employment and training, and set up self-development groups for business and social entrepreneurs who were finding the going tough and feeling isolated. He has worked for others and himself in management consultancy and in business, and has also experienced the trauma of redundancy.

In an economic and political climate in which neither business nor social innovators are encouraged to take risks, Brian sees hope in the number of people who slog away to create something from very little except their own determination to move mountains and overcome apathy. It is to these people that this book is dedicated.

Brian is now vicar of a large urban parish in Sheffield.

Why Self-Help?

> 'Many feel that full employment will not return within our lifetime.'*
>
> 'In the period 1964 to 1978 the five best-functioning industrial companies increased their production by an average of 76.3% but their employment declined by an average of 15%'**

Many of us think of an 'activist' as a member of a political group. We may not see ourselves as activists. But more and more of us are finding ourselves in a very active role, trying to start some new project for the unemployed in our community—school leavers, redundant workers, skilled craftsmen and women, or managers.

People who start such projects do not come from any one group in society. They may be a group of redundant steel workers living in the same district, or former executives or teachers. There may also be a paid adult education, social, or church worker.

Whoever they are, they have something in common. They all believe that:

- there is no magic wand to make much difference to the levels of unemployment for many years to come, so there will not be enough employment opportunities for everyone;

- if the community does not help itself, nobody else will;

---

*The Self-Help Economy, Knight & Hayes, London Voluntary Service Council, 1982.
**A Life to Live, Clemitson & Rodgers, Junction Books, 1981.

- in any case a successful project with local roots is more likely to keep going and will do more for the economic welfare and the morale of the whole community than many schemes brought in from outside.

It seems that we need to work to give our lives meaning, and to know who we are. In the past, work meant employment for most people. In the future, it may mean employment, or it may mean doing something for society for a reward which is not a traditional wage. What is certain is that the more projects are started locally, the more politicians will have to make these self-help efforts possible and rewarded, if they want the support of the electorate.

What this book is trying to do

This book is *not* going to analyse the causes of unemployment, and it is not going to suggest how the government might reduce the numbers out of work.

What it will try to do is:

- give practical guidelines for action, and information based on the experiences of various people who have set up self-help groups before;

- deal with questions which sooner or later any individual or group hoping to get a self-help project going—and keep it going!—will have to face;

- show how a community seldom accepts a new idea on merit. Organisers have to stimulate a sense of awareness of the needs and issues before they can achieve anything.

- suggest a variety of purposes and activities for starting a self-help project, and ways of working out decisions so that the members of the project and the community feel they are part of it, and learn from it.

What if you don't succeed?

Not every individual or group who sets off on this path succeeds in conventional terms. Some finish up with something that isn't much like they thought it would be when they started out. Some projects collapse because the very people the whole scheme depends on are also the most energetic and imaginative at job-seeking.

What most people have in common, whether they succeed or fold up, is that they learn a tremendous amount which stands them in good stead if they look for another job, if they become self-employed, or if they start another new project. At the very least, many find that the experience lifts them out of a 'no hope' feeling of depression and gives them something to live and work for.

A priest in Northern Ireland had to wind up a community set up to build a bridge between communities. Asked if he felt it had been worthwhile he replied: 'Better to light one candle than forever to curse the darkness'.

■1 Getting the Ball Rolling

Where to start?

> 'The longest journey begins with the first step.' (Chinese proverb)
>
> 'Like the Boss always says, however big the pile, you can only peel one potato at a time.' (Sunday afternoon T.V. Western)

Having some sort of check-list makes the goal seem possible. Working through the list gives a sense of achievement. So make a list for your group as you go along. Some items on the list you will find in the following chapters. Other items will be unique to your project.

What exists?

Finding out what is already happening is a very helpful way to start. It saves you trying to do what other people are doing and may help you see the gaps in existing activities. It may also provide you with a base to work from, or be a spring board for an extension.

For example, a group who were using an Adult Education Centre for an unemployed self-help education and training scheme formed a temporary co-operative to make certain products solely for the Christmas sales period.

An active group of high-rise flat dwellers tried unsuccessfully for several months to obtain small premises in a nearby block of empty shops owned by their Local Authority. They wanted to open it as a community and unemployed Drop-In Centre, with a café and information facilities.

200 yards away an Adult Education worker suddenly announced that some redundant school premises were opening for the same purpose, after an equally long struggle. Neither party knew of the existence of the other!

If you can find any of the following in your area, go and see them:

- Drop-In Centre
- Rights and Advice Centre
- Claimants Union
- Trade Union Resources Centre
- Job Swap or Skill Exchange Scheme
- Community Workshops
- Centre for the Unemployed

Or you may come across schemes already existing to create jobs under one of the Government schemes. The sort of people to contact about these are:

- Manpower Services Commission
- Age Concern
- N.S.P.C.C.
- Council for Voluntary Service
- Volunteer Bureau
- Industrial Mission chaplains and churches.

Reactions to your enquiries will vary. Some will show little more than polite interest, but people involved in these schemes are often aware of their potential elsewhere, and have ideas for what could be done. They also have a lot of contacts themselves. If they don't exist where you are, see if you can find out if they do nearby.

Arousing interest

A lot of organisations in the community contain people who are very concerned about unemployment. But they need prompting to put it in on their agenda so that their groups take action. Some of them may not want to be involved. Some may simply not have thought they had anything to offer.

Local churches are often very helpful, but why not approach

- *Parent Teacher Associations?* They are concerned about lack of jobs for school leavers and often have a lot of energy which can be harnessed. This does not need to detract from their normal activities—indeed it would raise their standing in the community.

- *Sports Clubs?* Many are affected by falling membership because of higher fees resulting from higher costs.

- *Working Men's or Social Clubs?* Many are very good at fund raising, and often have underused premises, especially in the day-time.

It's also worth taking the time to talk to your local

- Chamber of Commerce
- clergy in all churches
- social workers
- council officers
- local councillors
- club secretaries
- Adult Education workers
- Trades Council and Trade Union officials
- Working Co-operatives*

Public meeting

When you have started these groups or individuals thinking about what they could do, it might be a good idea to call a public meeting to bring together unemployed people in the community, with the representatives mentioned above, to stimulate further interest and energy.

Where? The local school may be a good place, but not always,

---

*The 'Directory of Industrial and Service Co-operatives' gives details of all co-operatives. See end of Chapter 7 for details.

especially if it has to charge. (If it does, and there is nowhere else, ask one of the local churches to donate the hire charge.) Another drawback is that people see a school as an 'official' place—and don't turn up.

A community or Adult Education centre, or a large room in a local pub often feels more like home territory to those you want to get there.

Publicity: Handmade posters in pubs, clubs and other hubs of society, such as shops or libraries, can be a help. Also advise local radio, newspapers and community leaders—e.g. clergy, social and Adult Education workers.

The meeting: The credibility of any future scheme is often judged by the way such a meeting is handled. A meeting that has a clear way of working, and somebody in the driving seat, is always viewed

7

as less time wasting than a rambling shouting match, often described as 'all heat and no light'!

Many groups believe it is very important to create democratic ways of working. But this has to be worked at, it does not just happen. It is not easy to arrange a large meeting, and there has to be some form of control.

Some useful hints

- If you are not used to running such meetings, get help from somebody who is. (See Chapter 10.)

- If you want to make a report or speech supporting some action or view to any extent, don't take the chair yourself. Or, you can vacate the chair while you make your point.

- For some people, getting a point of view expressed is more important than the outcome.

- Set a limited objective for the meeting, such as hearing views, taking names of interested people, nominating people in the community as sponsors or from whom a working group can seek advice.

- The first meeting will include a lot of people who are interested and want to show support, but not take an active part. Try to keep their names separate. Later you may be in a position to fund an information bulletin for them, or you may need them to show support again.

- If the meeting contains a lot of 'goodwill' supporters who will not be active, you may be better off not trying to elect a committee. Your *next* meeting is more likely to sort out those who actually want to do something, and if there are tasks for everyone, why have a committee too soon? Ask those present to prepare NOMINATIONS for a committee in time for the next meeting.

- See chapter 10 for further points and hints on this subject.

Purposes

During your investigations and at a public meeting you will find a variety of reactions, not all of them positive. Why? Different people will put different interpretations on the reason for your project, however you explain it, and whatever you call it. They will also have their own views, often strong ones, on what a self-help scheme ought to be. Exploring, combining and reconciling these views needs to be done sooner rather than later, or they may destroy the scheme quite early on. On the other hand, they may also widen the scheme beyond your original concept.

Working it out
The next chapter does two things:

1. It gives a brief description of the activities in some self-help groups, and suggests some of the aims of such groups.

2. It suggests a way in which a new group, with or without much experience, can start to work out their own aims and objectives.

2 Who and What Are We Here For?

> 'Having lost sight of our objectives, let us redouble our efforts.'

This could well be the slogan for a lot of voluntary groups and organisations. Many groups set out to do one thing and finish up doing something rather different, or carry out activities which become an end in themselves. It is a useful self-discipline for any group to sit down from time to time and ask two questions:

1. What are we trying to achieve? Who for?

This is *not* asking what you are doing by way of activities. It *is* asking 'What is your primary purpose, your reason for existence?' The activities are only the means for achieving them—the 'How'.

2. How are we trying to achieve this?

Why are we doing what we are doing? Is it going to move the group forward in trying to achieve its primary purpose?

Very often, a project thought up to meet one need also fulfils others, accidentally or on purpose. There is nothing wrong with that, but it is useful to be aware that it is happening.

•

Much of this chapter is written as if you are starting from scratch. It makes some assumptions about obtaining premises to do all the things you would like to do.

In reality, most of you who read this will either have something under way, which you are trying to build up, or you will have the offer of some facilities which may in themselves limit what you try to achieve.

Activities

The wheel below shows some of the main activities which people usually have in mind when they start a project for the unemployed. Some of the ideas may be unfamiliar, but they are well tried. Later chapters will describe each in more detail.

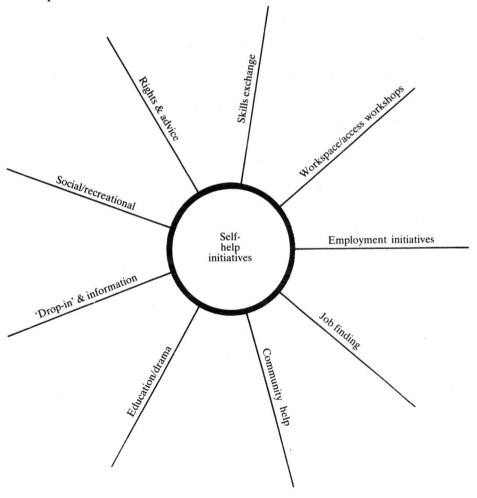

Explanation

Both these can mean whatever you want them to mean—there's no limit!

Now we will look at the activities shown on the wheel above:

Workspace/access workshops
Facilities which people can use free or for a 'cost only' fee. These may range from desks, typewriter, duplicator, telephone, typing or phone-answering services to a book-keeping service, business address record or computer. The workshop may range from a work bench with a vice and hand tools to a bandsaw, lathe or other equipment for use under supervision.

Employment and occupational initiatives
These could include: starting a co-operative enterprise, encouraging local people to set up on their own by offering space and facilities, or getting together small groups of people who have not met before and have no previous objectives, to work out ideas on flip-charts, i.e. large pads of newsprint hung up for use with a felt-tip pen.

Job finding
This usually means finding people with training and experience to help others to write effective applications or to complete forms, plus training in being interviewed or counselling for retraining. It may also include approaching firms 'cold'.

Community help
Putting unemployed or underemployed people with skills or spare

time in touch with community groups who need their help. For example, book-keeping, fund-raising, secretarial work.

Education/drama
Making use of the skills and knowledge of members by passing them on to others. Using drama to educate or to highlight current local issues.

'Drop-in' and information
Often the hub of activities, where local people can meet, exchange ideas, put up notices, give and receive information in an informal and relaxed way. Often includes a coffee bar, cafeteria, notice boards and administrative help.

Social/recreational
Anything from table tennis, a darts or football team, to outings by coach or train.

Rights and advice centre
An information desk with clued up volunteers or paid staff, where people with problems over DHSS or unemployment benefits can receive unbiased advice in confidence.

Skills exchange
A facility through which people offer and receive free help. It encourages local people to help each other on the basis that everybody in a community has something to offer, even if only sitting and listening.

Looking ahead. It is often a good idea to start with limited facilities for limited objectives, such as a Drop-in and Information, Rights and Advice Centre (with a coffee bar included). But looking further ahead at this stage will give you a picture of long-term plans—yours and other's. It may help you not to seize the first building available, which could turn out to have no scope for additional activities which you may want to introduce later.

Statement of intent

Sitting down and working out a statement of intent sounds a fearful drudge and time wasting. It may not be easy—but it is not wasted. Having it set down and publicised can help you in several ways:

- It can make it clear what you are not trying to do as well as what you are. There may be people who think the project will be a threat to them—nearby home dwellers, local traders and licensees, political groups. Your statement of intent will help set their minds at rest.

- It makes sure that if your initiating group or supporters (like a local councillor or vicar) make statements to others, such as local residents, the press or radio, they say the same thing and don't make assumptions.

- The statement can attract the interest of people who might use your facilities, and it will be a 'hook' on which others can hang their ideas.

Sample statement of intent

We are a group of residents in the Wash Green area who want to start a community Self-help scheme. We have made applications to the local authority for the use of the former Bath Houses on Long Lane.

We have no cut and dried plans at this stage (and no money!). We want anybody who is interested and is prepared to help to have their say. We hope to provide a facility for all age groups, especially for the unemployed and underemployed, where they can meet, relax, support each other in job-hunting or creating new enterprises, and finding new ways of living their lives, both for themselves and the local community.

We will not be opening licensed bars or holding frequent discos. We will not be competing with local traders. Basically we hope to provide a facility where long- or short-term unemployed or underemployed can keep in touch with each other and the community, and find ways of helping themselves and the community.

This statement can be distributed to local churches, social centres, sports clubs, public libraries, post offices and newsagents' notice boards.

Who are we here for?

When groups get going they usually say, 'This is for the unemployed'. Eventually they find their scope widens. They include unregistered unemployed, underemployed, semi, early or fully retired, and then anybody in the community who has spare time and talents to contribute. Sometimes people in regular employment have a particular talent or professional skill which you need. Experience has shown that:

- many people who want to work now realise that work may not mean employment, but is worth doing, and that money is not the only reward;

- most people are not 'scroungers'; they want to contribute something and to be with other people, whether they are skilled or unskilled;

- people who have skills want to use them to stop them rusting, and for their own satisfaction. Not everybody can use all their skills in a conventional job. That's why many people work voluntarily.

'Who are we here for?' is a question worth asking several times:

- on starting up, to help others realise the group need not be exclusive;
- after starting, to remind yourselves what it is all about;
- when you've been running for a while, to look around to see if a small 'clique' has taken over which is excluding others.

Each group has to work out its own reasons for existence. Some common ones are:

Typical objectives

- To help ourselves as long-term and short-term underemployed men, women and young people;

- to keep in contact and support each other;
- to find ways of helping others in the community—young school leavers, the retired, and the elderly;
- to be in charge of our own lives and to make better use of our lives;
- to provide a social base from which to operate.

Gaining a vision

As we saw at the end of Chapter 1, the people who have the energy and drive to try to start a project are bound to have fairly strong views on what it should look like and how people should see it. These views can be contradictory. For example, some people may want to concentrate on trying to find ways of earning a living; some may want to use the project to launch political action against unemployment. Both may be legitimate activities, but not everybody may be equally happy with them.

People's aims will not always be the same, even when they are all 'on the table'. When they are not aired, for whatever reason, life becomes even more difficult. So let's look at some ways of getting things out on the table—your own ideas and other people's:

Verbal methods

1. Ask each member of the group to write down on a piece of paper what they want from the project. Ask them to begin each statement with the words 'How to . . .' They can write as many as they like. Give them 5 minutes or so to think about it. Do your own list.

2. Use a long piece of poster paper and a felt tip pen. Go round the group and ask each person to read out one of their statements, and write it up. Keep going around until all the statements are listed. If they are very similar, tick the one already listed, and add to it if necessary.

3. Go through the statements and mark the list to group together similar statements. For example, group statements to do with

    social services   helping the community
    business or co-operatives   helping people to find jobs

4. Go through the statements again to see if any of them are in conflict. If they are the group must resolve them by negotiation at an early stage. For example, 'how to act non-politically' may conflict with 'how to support Trades Council demonstrations against unemployment'.

Visual methods

Quite a lot of people are not very good at putting things into words. So, here are three ways a group can have some fun and express their thoughts visually. They do not need to be artists! Any of these could be a warm up for the verbal exercise given above.

Collages Each person needs a sheet of plain paper, several old newspapers and/or magazines, a pair of scissors and a pot of glue. Ask them to cut out and paste on to the paper any picture or phrase that says something of what they hope the project will be about.

When everyone has finished, the group talks with each member in turn about his collage and what it says. The group then writes up the key words from each presentation, e.g. 'open all hours', 'welcoming'.

Posters Each person has a piece of plain paper and some coloured wax crayons or felt tip pens. The paper should not be less than small poster size (approx. 455 × 300mm). The object is to produce a poster advertising the centre to others. Again, when completed, examine each in turn and write up key words.

Pictures The same equipment as for the posters. Ask people to draw a picture showing the sort of centre or project they want. Discuss and summarise as before.

If possible, pin up all the pictures, posters or collages on a wall or board, and have another look at them later. Get other people to comment on them. A second look often shows things which were missed on the first look and discussion.

Priorities

It's easy to talk about setting priorities. In reality we tend to do what can be done and get on with it. Even so, it does help to list all the things that have to be done, and add to the list every time somebody thinks up something new.

As each item on the list is completed, cross it off and make a separate note of what you did, who said or promised what, and the date. Go over the list daily and mark it:

Mark A: items on which action must be taken soonest;
Mark B: items which can wait.

After each item mark who is responsible for doing it. For example:

A Book hall for meeting—John
B Write to charities, churches, etc.—George
B Contact post office—Roger
A Design door-to-door handbills for printers—Jane
A Posters for shop, P.O., etc.—Jane
B See Estate Surveyor re building—John
B Meet Chamber of Trade secretary—Roger
A See Vicar re basement—John
B Ring Housing Department re letting—Roger
B Local radio, press—Jane

Finally in this chapter, two points to think about.

1. Whose project is it?

'My experience nearly broke up my family. I had to get my phone number changed.'

(Unemployed Community Initiator)

'The group became so dependent on my running around, and my support, I had to ask for a transfer to another Adult Education base. People were ringing up at 2 am.'

(Adult Education worker.)

Both these workers started out with a high commitment to a co-operative way of working and were very much against paternalism. Yet both finished up doing just the opposite to what they set out to do. Very often people with the drive to get something going start off by thinking:

'I'll do the spadework and then hand over to the others'.
'It's more reliable and quicker if I do things myself.'

It is often true that people who have been unemployed for some time lack self-confidence and can't see any possibility of 'self-help'. But the chasing around and spadework will get them to turn out and do something. This is much better than doing things for them. Otherwise it becomes just another scheme somebody is doing 'for them'.

The truth of this will be seen more clearly if the person with the drive packs up. Usually people with this sort of drive are the very ones who are most energetic at finding themselves a job. This leaves the rest floundering and the whole project may fall through.

> Individual 'take-overs' can also be a menace. A 'sew and sell' co-operative found that one member of its committee, the treasurer, was making decisions she was not responsible for—refusing to pay for items she thought unnecessary, interfering in the decisions of sub-committees. She was eventually removed by bringing in a 2-year rule, that all office-holders must change every 2 years.

2.   It takes time to build a team

People join a group with different expectations. Some will be half-hearted and may make you despondent. Others will want to take it over themselves and feel you are too slow.

If you want to build a working team you have to build up trust. This takes time, and everyone must have a chance to have their say, get to know one another, and be a part of some success. The exercises described earlier will help, but before starting there are other contributions you can make:

- Spend some time letting people get to know each other. This can be done either by each person spending 2 minutes telling the rest of the group who they are, where they are from and so on, *or* by splitting into pairs, spending 5 minutes each telling the other person about yourself (= 10 minutes). Then the other person introduces you to the rest of the group. This is sometimes comfortable for people who don't like talking to groups about themselves.

- Don't make it look as though you have all the answers. It will put others off. Express your concerns, not your solutions.

    For example, you might say:

    'I've been made redundant once—I don't want to be in a

position where I'm dependent on other people making decisions about my future again. What can we do?'

This is very different from saying:

'I've got this idea for making wooden toys for Christmas' to which others might respond, "good for you—get on with it!"

or

'St Marks church has got a spare basement. How can we make best use of it for the unemployed?'

This is very different from saying:

'I've measured up St. Marks basement. We could get a small bandsaw and a work bench in there for a workshop. Now if you and you will go around to see if you can scrounge some tools . . .' which leaves the rest feeling they are only carrying out your priorities.

- Having an early success is important to everybody, it keeps them going. Some charities respond very quickly to appeals for funds. Aim to do something practical as soon as possible.

- Have fun doing it! If it gets too 'heavy' some people will decide they get enough of that at home.

Some examples of basic questions which have arisen when setting objectives are:

- To what extent will the activity be set or controlled by sponsors or a 3rd party such as the MSC? Can the group satisfy their requirements and maintain its integrity?

- Will the activity separate unemployed from the rest of the community, and if so why?

- Will activities be life enhancing, giving people more insight into their own capabilities and self respect?

- In an age when we have more time on our hands than ever will the activity enhance people's ability to use it more creatively? Will it provide the 'instant' product—games, music and food, or help people think about what they cook and eat, how they play, make music, or create items which are useful or ornamental? And will their music only continue to echo the sense of despair and failure heard in the lyrics of teenage pop?

- If young people are to use the activity will the adult leadership around them give hope and encouragement and maturity in the face of pessimism? What a teenager most wants to learn in life, is not how to be a teenager but an adult.

- Will any new activity be controlled and sustained by local energy and resources, or will it be vulnerable to decisions taken by people elsewhere which could bring it to a halt, e.g. MSC, or Local Authority?

- Will the activity have any influence on other members of the community? Will it influence the affluent and educate them, or will it provide cheap services for them? Will it carry out jobs which have traditionally been undertaken voluntarily?

- Is the activity truly 'self-help' and likely to create a sense of community achievement, or is it dependent on paid managers or sponsors' initiatives? If so, is this acceptable?

- Will the project care for those least able to help themselves, i.e. the sick, handicapped, children, prisoners, unemployed, deprived, or poor?

- Will the activities reduce divisions in society which separate people or communities from each other, or generate attitudes of superiority or deference?

- Will people be encouraged to have more say over their daily lives and the life of society—fostering training and leadership development for those who in the past have been passive recipients?

- Will those involved be encouraged to think about and work for change in policies about local transport, jobs, schools, health facilities, shops, or leisure, benefits and rights whether from local or national government?

Old power or new power? A word of caution

One characteristic of many schemes (both official and self-help) is that they finish up achieving precisely the opposite to what they intended.

For example, community groups may not be set up to create jobs, but to stimulate and involve local people. This often means that an existing group, which may seem conservative or reactionary, has its nose put out of joint. And because community participation and consultation is slow and often difficult—even painful—the new group finishes up as the new autocratic power centre. They believe they know what is best for everyone else, and the community is just as alienated from them and just as apathetic towards their activities as they ever were.

Another example is in activities known as 'Drop-In Centres'. Colin Walker of Gateshead CVS found in a survey that what started as a caring 'First Aid' activity amounted to little more than adult youth clubs in which people were trapped in what he called the 'pool and darts syndrome'. They segregated the unemployed from the community in a way not of their own choosing and discriminated against women and older men by their limited facilities. This left groups of young men in isolation and with strong sexist attitudes.

So,

- take some time to sort out what it is you're hoping to achieve by the activities you undertake

- keep reviewing whether your original objectives are too broad or too narrow

- take a hard look, at least once a year, at whether what you are doing ties in with what you set out to do.

I shall refer to this subject again at intervals.

▣ A Roof Over Our Heads

A A community group raised and spent several thousand pounds on renovating a building for self-help and employment activities. They then received advice from the Fire Prevention Officer that their plans showed change of use in the building which would involve access by the public. This required more stringent fire prevention and escape facilities than had been allowed for, and the project had to be abandoned.

B The trustees of an educational charity located premises which were then approved by the Fire Prevention Officer, Technical Adviser of the Manpower Services Commission, relevant Local Authority building and planning regulations officers, and the Health and Safety executive as suitable for a small foundry training workshop for unemployed youngsters. Fortunately, before they spent any money, an experienced foundryman seconded by a large company pointed out some basic flaws in their plans, and fire risks which the others had not appreciated.

If you look at the agenda for any self-help group just starting up, certain fundamental subjects crop up every time. One of these is 'Premises'. Together with 'funds' they constitute the main limiting or enabling factor in putting any scheme together. The two examples quoted above illustrate two important points:

1. It is important to get expert help at the earliest possible stage. There are increasing numbers of agencies and cash sources to help with this, which we will look at later in this chapter.

2. Even when you think you've got it right, generalised advisers may not have all the answers, and advice from a specialist architect, or somebody with actual experience in the activity which you hope to carry out, can pay off.

'The Council should do something'

Very often it is not difficult to identify an empty building owned by a local authority. Some have notice boards advertising the property to let by the Council. Others are known to have been used by specific departments, such as Education. Seeing such property empty (and often vandalised), it is natural to conclude that the authority will welcome an approach by a community group to keep it in good repair in return for a 'peppercorn rent'.

Unfortunately, local authorities do not work like that! Every department, including the Estates Department responsible for allocating property, is responsible to the district auditor, who has a responsibility to the ratepayers.

All property used has to be paid for by somebody. So if the local authority wants to make a building available to a community group, funds have to be allocated for the purpose. There have been situations where a department has allowed a group to use a building for a nominal rent, only to be overruled later by the Estates department demanding back rent!

Finding a place

It often takes some footslogging to find good premises, but there are some short cuts. You could:

- Contact the Small Firms Information Service.

- Approach the Council's Planning Development Officer, Industrial Development Officer, or equivalent (part of their job is to give advice and support); the Planning Officer may have a list of vacant buildings.

- Approach your local councillor and get him to support your approach to the Council. Local authorities now often give priority to any proposal likely to create jobs.

  Don't be put off by the Estates Department saying that nothing is available. In present economic conditions this is unlikely to be true. Such a reply often means that the

department concerned does not want to get involved in the rather 'messy' business of dealing with a community group.

- Approach estate agents. Don't be put off by rents quoted. If the premises are suited to your needs several possibilities may present themselves:

  (a) if the premises have been empty for some time, the landlords may be glad of an offer that keeps the building from deteriorating;

  (b) if the building is an old one, it may be virtually unlettable, in which case the owners may welcome any approach;

(c) If your scheme qualifies for assistance from the local authority or one of the Government schemes, the rent may be taken care of.

Don't expect too much professional competence from agents. Some are very helpful, but once you are on their circulation list the fact that you have asked for, say, a convertible property of approx. 100 square metres in Postal District 6, won't prevent them sending you details of anything from a new residential bungalow in District 10 to 1,000 square metres of factory space in District 14!

Merry footslogging!

Finally, have as many people as possible looking for empty buildings—and not just those with signs outside. There are many buildings fully or partially empty which are not advertised at all. Councils have registers of rate-payers for all properties, so you should be able to find out who owns or administers any empty building, whether it is the Council or a private owner.

Some firms have 'shrunk' and only use part of their premises, but have not sought to let off the rest. It's worth approaching them.

Promises, promises

At a conference run by the National Council of Voluntary Organisations on the role of local authorities in creating community resources from vacant buildings, a delegate gave the following advice:

- Don't be taken in by promises of 'jam tomorrow' if you'll accept a temporary move now.

- If you know that a good building is becoming vacant, act quickly. There is often competition, if only from bulldozers. Make a written 'statement of intent' to all and sundry as a first step.

- Don't believe anybody who says there is nothing available. Keep knocking and kicking the door to get it open.

- If you are applying for a grant for premises, make sure you get some technical advice first, *before* submitting your application. Only a few councils have officers specially briefed with the time to help you prepare an application that satisfies various regulations.

- Don't rely on promises. Act as if *nothing* is happening until something *does* happen.

- Keep pressing councillors or the local authority's officers to keep your problem on the agenda. The less fuss there is, the less likelihood there is of anything happening.

What is involved? (or 'What are we letting ourselves in for?')

We can't go into all the building legalities and responsibilities in this book. It all looks more difficult on paper than it is, but there are pitfalls for the unwary.

The best publication on the subject is *Getting Started* by Coventry City Council, Coventry V.S. Council, Tudor House, 14 Spoon Street, Coventry CV1 3BA.

The following are just a few notes of introduction and guidelines.

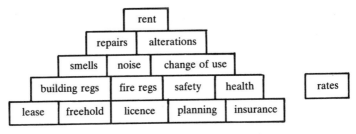

Once you start to even look for premises, there are some things you have to know. But even if you don't you soon learn! One of the best ways to avoid pitfalls is to co-opt somebody with some experience with buildings—especially anyone using a building for community purposes.

Here are a few of the more basic bits of information, which apply whether you are buying, borrowing or squatting!

Purchase, lease or licence?

Purchase

Whatever you intend, get legal advice. If you can find a community lawyer so much the better, otherwise approach the Citizens Advice Bureau. Buying is usually expensive and outside the means of a small new organisation. However, if you come within a Government or local authority scheme which would pay your rent, you may find them prepared to pay out the same money for purchasing. In this case you use the grant money to repay a bank loan or mortgage.

Lease

This is the term used for an agreement between an owner (public or private) and a prospective tenant. There are so many interpretations and legal meanings to a lease that legal help is essential. If you intend spending money on improvements, make sure the lease is renewable at the end of the term fixed (e.g. 5-year lease). The Landlord and Tenant Act ensures that rents cannot be raised too dramatically on a new lease, and that you cannot be evicted easily, in just the same way as it does for private housing (except on very short-term leases, such as pre-demolition).

Licence

This is much simpler than a lease and there is usually a fixed notice period—a week, a month or 3 months. Licences are often used in 'Work-space' buildings (explained elsewhere). There is less legal protection than with a lease, but on the other hand you don't have to find more than the agreed minimum notice of rent if you want to pull out in a hurry.

Planning and building regulations

A good reason to get expert help *before* acquiring premises, by whatever means, is to make sure you know what alterations or repairs are necessary before you sign anything, and assess their costs. Also a lease may have a clause preventing you from using the building for certain activities, or altering it the way you want.

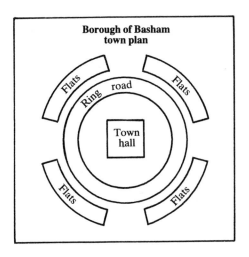

**Borough of Basham
town plan**

Flats

Ring road

Flats

Town
hall

Flats

Flats

Planning permission

This is normally needed only if the proposed work only affects the *exterior* of a building, or if it involves change of use—e.g. changing shops into offices, or dividing up a house. Always check with your local Planning Department—it costs nothing.

Basically, the procedure is straightforward and town hall planning officials will often give advice and support, especially if your scheme will help provide even one or two jobs. The sooner you get your application in, the better. You may be in a hurry—but planning processes cannot be unduly hurried. Allow 2–3 months. Usually a fee is charged: the planners will give you details.

Love Your Neighbour!

I've mentioned it before, but it's worth repeating. Other local people can raise objections and squash your idea at birth—even though they don't understand it. The Planning Department will be more helpful if you can show that you have consulted the local community and have them on your side. You can achieve this by

- trying out ideas on local residents;
- getting them to help search for premises;
- using a local questionnaire.

Building regulations

Any alterations or extensions of almost any consequence need the consent of the Building Regulations Inspector *whether or not planning permission is needed.* An inspector of this department usually inspects work as it is in progress, to make sure it is up to standard. If you act without permission you are breaking the law and you will probably be ordered to pull down whatever you have put up!

Health and safety

Every area has an Environmental Health Officer to make sure that any premises where people are employed comply with the Offices, Shops and Railway Premises Act of 1963.

Local bylaws cover such things as: lavatories, washing facilities and drinking water; lighting and ventilation; temperatures, fumes and smells; cleanliness and overcrowding; and machinery.

Public health legislation is specially concerned with clean and fouled air; all aspects of food handling, preparation and storage, whether for social reasons or sale; housing and sanitary standards; working conditions; licensing for alcohol or activities; waste and drainage; infection and other diseases; and pests and vermin.

When a building is open to the public, fire precautions are much more stringent than for a private building. Your local Fire Prevention officer is available to advise you on such matters as escape routes, equipment and alarms, and emergency doors.

30

Insurance
Get some advice from a reliable broker on what sort of insurance is best for your group. Ask him what steps to take to avoid damage or theft. Ask what conditions the insurance companies may require before accepting insurance or paying out.

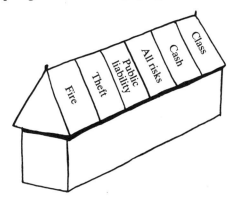

We're in!
Once you have a building, it's very important for the morale of the community and those involved in the project to use it as quickly as possible. Even if you have no gas, water or electricity, get people inside to make some use of it, however limited.

Rates
If your organisation registers as a charity you will be entitled to rent rebate as of right (50 per cent at the time of writing). Some councils give further rebates.

Government and local authority help
The Urban Initiatives Fund was set up as part of the Department of Environment's Small Grants Programme, and is available 'to national and regional voluntary bodies wishing to undertake programmes through which people can better understand and shape their environment'. Each year a sum is earmarked to meet 50 per cent of the cost of providing specialist advice, including management advice to voluntary groups setting up building rehabilitation and site clearance projects in urban areas.

One of the groups receiving funds under this scheme is the Inter Action Trust Ltd. This was founded to stimulate community involvement and encourage a creative approach and mutual help projects in neighbourhoods.

The 'Neighbourhood Use of Buildings and Space' (NUBS) is a specialist division of Inter Action Trust Ltd which works with voluntary agencies. Its aim is to develop derelict land and buildings in the inner city for the benefit of local communities, particularly for groups with special needs. NUBS will give up to 40 hours work free of charge to community groups with no funds to pay fees. For others, there is a flexible fee depending on ability to pay. Contact

NUBS, 15 Wilkin Street,
London NW5. Tel. 01-267 9421

How the Local Authority can act (or how to be an active activist)

The funds described above are just one example of many types of funding now available. Some local authorities have cottoned on to this fact and have set up advisory units of their own. These cost the ratepayer very little as they use these funds and others such as the Manpower Services Commission. Such a unit can help make the whole process less cumbersome and daunting. It can provide information, unblock departmental or individual hold-ups in the Town Hall, and bring to the Council's notice any gaps in policy which prevent action.

Most important of all it means that a community group with initiative is not dependent on an ad hoc decision of Council or on the assistance of one or two councillors with a bit more clout than others!

If your Local Authority has no such unit, why not approach them and get other voluntary groups to do the same? If you have a local Council for Voluntary Services they would be a useful body to assist. Specifically local authorities can be pressed for:

- a statement of commitment to a policy of leasing;
- availability of short-life property for community use;
- guidance on obtaining planning permission and other statutory requirements;

- support for management training schemes for groups developing and having to manage property;
- suggestions as to how facilities can be shared to maximise community use, rather than allowing premises to be idle for long periods;
- special measures to promote the involvement of less professional groups, such as ethnic minorities and young people, in the care and management of buildings;
- information via leaflets, libraries and lay voluntary organisations describing which council departments and officers can provide assistance on acquisitions, funding and operating buildings and premises.

Dealing with the Local Authority

The majority of people in Local Government offices are very helpful. However there is a code which some of them slip into which it is as well to know exists. After a while you could write your own Local Authority Dictionary based on your own experiences. Here are some examples:

- 'This will have to go before committee' *means* 'I have to find out if you have any friends whom I can't afford to upset.'

- 'What is your constituency?' *means* 'Just because you've a good idea don't assume it cuts any ice here. Clout is what matters.'

- 'How does this fit into our corporate plan?' *means* 'Who's backing you? What will the Councillors think?'

- 'No suitable premises available' *means* 'We may have nearly two million square metres of unused office and factory space on our hands but unless you can find a department to pay the rent you can't have it!'

4 Involving the Community

'Why should people around here be interested? Some of them belong to different clubs, choral societies and organisations already. The ones most likely to be useful are probably already busy.'

Much of this is true, of course. But we must realise that the future of voluntary societies and clubs, and even organisations such as Scouts, Guides, or Boys Brigade, is often directly connected with there continuing to be a number of paid jobs or voluntary work available in the community. So in their own interest, for their survival as a community, people should support attempts to start new activities which will enable residents to stay in the area each day, whether in a voluntary or a paid job. Why is this?

Immigrant Labour

Talk about 'immigrant labour' and most people think of countries like South Africa or West Germany. But centralisation of our own factories and offices in large towns means that people of working age and ability are either drawn to live in the suburbs of larger towns or move to rural communities. They may travel long distances to work. Fewer people work in their own home districts than travel away. So their home areas, whether urban or rural, become mere dormitories.

Dormitory Suburbs

In south-east England about 60–70 per cent of the inhabitants of many villages have moved into them from urban areas. This has also happened in semi-urban and rural areas around cities and towns like Sheffield, Manchester, Birmingham or Bristol. At one time the majority of people who lived in villages worked in the farms, quarries, mills or trades, or they were self-employed craftsmen such as blacksmiths, shoemakers or carpenters. Now, most of those in work commute elsewhere, and old skills disappear.

Older inhabitants of town suburbs which used to be villages can tell you that, 'Mr Jones used to make and repair shoes in that building at the back of the library that's now a hairdresser's'; or 'Mum and the family used to make a few shillings in the summer picking potatoes in that field where the new estate is.' In other words, not all the work in the community was cut off from the rest of its life by those in work catching the 7.45 a.m. each morning and returning at night.

This division of home and work has several effects:

- some places finish up with an unbalanced population, overweighted either with young couples with small children, or with the elderly;
- when most breadwinners are commuting, local shops suffer when commuters take advantage of large store prices and a wider range of goods in the town near their workplace;
- as the numbers of commuters increase, work and home begin to have fewer links; 'neighbourliness' is lost as the people next door become less well known to each other.

The drain on a community builds up when people's minds and interests become more set on the big city than on their local community. They contribute less to voluntary projects and social activities, and young people look for their social life outside.

We cannot put the clock back. Some people, probably a lot, will have to commute to work and there is no reason why they shouldn't. But levels of really local employment and neighbourliness do affect levels of voluntary activities in the community. So although they do have shortcomings, I believe that community-based schemes are worth while, and the MSC community programmes and voluntary projects are worth continuing and using, with certain reservations.

Using patrons and sponsors

A one-parent family group in high-rise flats set up a continuing committee after the success of their 'street party'. Following a complaint, believed to have been from a jealous tenant, the CID visited the committee to investigate how the funds were administered. The Treasurer said later that the Police backed off fairly quickly when they discovered that a local solicitor was on the committee. Unfortunately, damage was done by headlines in the local paper, and was never fully repaired.

It is sad but true that people often put confidence in titles rather than in competence. Even if they cannot play an active part, the names of local doctors, clergymen, councillors, Trade Union secretaries, solicitors or other professionals on your letterhead, as patron, sponsor or president, carry their own message to the community. The fact that such people are behind the activity, in spirit if not in presence, tells people that the project carries some weight and is in responsible hands.

But their roles need not just be prestigious. The support of professionals can reassure people who might be nervous about becoming involved. For example, knowing that a union official is backing you may be useful if somebody is worried that the project might be seen as a cheap labour scheme. A local doctor might find out about the numbers of elderly or invalids in the area more quickly than you, as a member of the general public, could do. The local gossip in pubs, clubs and other hubs of social activity is also more interesting when such people are included, ensuring good verbal publicity.

Who knows? Who wants to know? Who needs to know?

Whatever efforts you make at publicity, there will always be people who say they've never heard a thing about it. But imaginative publicity doesn't have to be expensive.

Questionnaires

One way of getting known, and finding out where people are and what they want is by using a door-to-door questionnaire, preceded by a notice advising people you are coming. Here is an example of a pamphlet:

I'M SICK OF THIS!

IF I HAD MY WAY THINGS WOULD BE DIFFERENT...

YOU COULDN'T BE MORE RIGHT

There's going to be someone coming round the houses in this area with a questionnaire on Thursday and Friday. This survey is to find out what people who are around in the daytime in this area would like to see going on. It could be anything from badminton to bingo, from a baby-sitting circle to free, open workshops or help and advice for local co-ops, etc.

The only way to find anything out is to ask, so that's what we're doing. So, if you want *your* say in what goes on round here from the Autumn onwards, here's your chance.

Note: There is one serious fault in this pamphlet. By law, any printing for public distribution must carry the names of the publisher (the person or group who issued it) and printer.

Although it helps to find out what people want, doing so is not all that straightforward:

- many people don't know what they want, so you must do your homework; then you can ask the type of question that attracts notice and pinpoints issues;

- you need a lot of volunteers and legwork to get round the neighbourhood to distribute advance notices and to ask the questions;

- volunteers can become very discouraged at the sheer apathy many people show towards a community activity—especially the young unemployed. On the other hand even the occasional enthusiastic response can lift you up again.

Advance notices

The advantage of putting round a pamphlet saying when you are coming is that when somebody answers the door you have a ready opening gambit:

> 'Good evening—I'm calling about the blue poster that was put through your door last week, explaining that we are opening a new community room at the old slaughter house.'

Also, it gives the impression of a well planned visit for a useful purpose, and shows a competent operation. A random call could raise suspicions that you may be up to no good.

Other publicity methods

Posters

Do remember the slogan KISS: 'Keep It Simple, Stupid!' Many posters suffer from basic defects such as

- being overloaded with information: the more diluted the message, the less it will be read;
- the print is too small: some posters will be read in shops or clubs close-to, but a lot will be in front windows of houses, so you must be able to read them from anything between 3.5 m and 10 m away;
- they lack punch, design and good layout.

Local radio

Both BBC and independent radio stations will usually give you at least one free announcement.

Press

If you can put together your information so as to make it a news item, both newspapers and free sheets will use it as long as they receive it in good time, typed and properly set out. Any publicity can be good publicity. Newspapers are particularly interested in stories of success or setbacks, complaints or objections to your scheme from local residents, or comments by a council or committee member. People have been known to invent or enlarge such stories just for the sake of publicity!

Have a Press Officer

If you appoint one of your members to be Press Officer you will gain in several ways:

- The local media will know who to contact if any news comes up involving your group.
- The media will come to know the person concerned and may be less inclined to believe stories that emanate from unofficial sources that don't seem to 'fit' what they know about you.
- The media staff will come to appreciate your help in obtaining copy—i.e. material which they can use from a reliable source.

Your choice of Press Officer is important as he or she will be dependent on relationships for credibility. Some groups have been sabotaged by 'spies' from opposing camps attending their meetings then rushing out to make statements of a 'shock/horror/crisis' type to the media. These are much harder to deny or counter once printed. If your Press Officer is known by name, face and phone number before this can happen, you have some chance of preventing it.

(See Chapter 6 for the examples from CHUG South Yorkshire).

Stalls

Hardly a week goes by in some places without a bring and buy, jumble sale, summer or winter fair. A word with the organisers may get you a stall where you can put up posters, give out leaflets, and have a chance to discuss your project with a captive audience. It would not be tactful to try and raise funds at the same event, but there is nothing to stop you holding your own fund-raising, later.

The great trick in any venture is always to act and speak not in terms of 'if' or 'we hope to', but as if you are already a going concern. If you can include a photograph or two of somebody *doing* something in a brochure, or even drawings of activities in a poster, they give the impression of action and purpose.

Some don't like it hot!

Franklin D. Roosevelt, a former President of the United States, is reported as having told a delegation for reform, 'Okay, you've convinced me—now go out and put pressure on me!' There is a real principle here: no administrator or politician can ignore an issue if you make it hot enough.

What Roosevelt said shows that reasoned arguments and logical goodwill are not enough to get what you want. The only way to get movement is to attack apathy.

A pressure group enables MPs, councillors or the decision-makers in local or national government to assess the degree of interest and support which exists for an issue. It can also stimulate healthy debate.

Of course, all change means *disorganisation* of the old and *organisation* of the new. The organiser's task is to seek out dissatisfaction and discontent and provide a channel into which people can pour their frustrations. This also drains off people's guilt for having put up with things for so long. Out of this arises a new organisation, a new form.

It might be said that a community does not have 'issues', although it could well have a bad scene, low self-esteem, a resignation that the world is against it, and a hope that someone, sometime, will do something about it.*

The organiser's first job is to create the issues and to identify problems. Through action, persuasion, asking questions, and

---

* Saul Alinsky, *Rules for Radicals,* Random House, New York.

communication he must make it clear that organising the community will give it power, activity and drive to do something about specific problems. A single issue is not enough. You can't maintain enough action on one issue, and an organisation needs action, otherwise it dies through argument, division and limited appeal.

Things happen for people who make things happen

The conclusion we can draw is this. Nobody is going to come round and ask you to start something to improve the amenities in your area, nor will you get bouquets for trying. You will have to help people see that there are problems and issues that can be tackled and solved, and then you will have to persuade them that *they* can do something about it. But you have to go out and do it. It's no use sitting back and waiting.

Des Wilson, former Director of Shelter has said that one of the first things the establishment will do is to test your persistence. If you don't like hard work don't get involved.

Management committees

Sooner or later—probably sooner—you will need to form a committee—a council, steering group or management committee. I shall discuss how to run a committee later on. Some important factors to think about are the following:

- Make up your mind if you are having a committee or a full membership meeting. If it is too small it may not be representative; if it is large, those left out may be resentful. It may be best at first to have a small group of people who are prepared to work.

- Time spent getting to know one another is never wasted. People trying to work together who are strangers take longer to achieve their business as the level of trust is too low, and the unstated 'hidden agenda' is not brought out into the open.

- It is very easy for the whole agenda of such a group to be taken up with *admin* rather than *issues*. By *admin* I mean such things as the budget or accounts, where to hold meetings, or how to get publicity. An *issue* is, for example, the apathy of unemployed young people in the area towards not only your project but any project, training scheme or educational self-improvement activity.

- Officials tend to like everybody and everything to fit neatly under labels. So when you want premises for a self-help scheme, for example, you are likely to be met with 'Ah—now will this be under the Education, Housing or Employment Creation Department?'

So authorities tend not to like, and find it hard to cope with

- groups which don't fit exactly under one label—e.g. a tenants' group trying out an adult education or job creation activity (that's Housing and Employment or Education!);
- short-life co-operatives, commercial or other ventures which can't show a willingness or a capacity for long-term survival and expansion;
- voluntary groups which get together for a particular purpose (e.g. the street party committee) and which they see as 'untidy'.

Not every new group or scheme meets such problems in officialdom, but it is as well to be prepared, or your project can be killed at birth. People who have the power to fund new schemes may be unable or unwilling to be flexible.

On the other hand, some officials have given and will continue to give every encouragement to new projects. So it's important (1) to be sure of your purpose, and (2) to keep up the pressure for change—often against highly patronising people who think they know what is best for others.

Meanwhile, see if you can get hold of a copy of *Management Committees* by Warren Feek from The National Youth Bureau, 17–23 Albion Street, Leicester LE1 6GD.

Other opposition

It's not just officials that may not be too keen on your new project or experiment. For every new group that starts up there are two others which will react as if they have the monopoly on community care or sole rights to the unemployed. 'Everybody's trying to get in on the act nowadays' said a member of a so-called 'caring profession' to me as he scornfully dismissed the activities of another initiative.

While one might expect such a reaction from some political purists, it is less welcome from local authorities, church agencies or individuals or other voluntary groups. If we are that threatened by another new idea we need to examine our own motives. You may of course be justified if it is unnecessary duplication and competition for limited resources.

Learn to learn

To me, the most important aspect of any community project is the opportunities it gives for all its members to learn to learn: to make sense out of their relationships to each other, to the project or scheme, and to the outside world. I have been involved in setting up a youth training workshop, and I have worked beside and talked to people involved in street parties, jazz clubs and computer classes, community workshops and taxis for the disabled. I have learnt more from them than from 90 per cent of the 'management' courses I have attended or run. And I know many people have been amazed at what they have done, and their lives have been enriched by their participation in a self-help group of some sort.

5 Voluntary Work

June and Richard are in their 60s. 2 days a week they help bring elderly housebound people to a luncheon club at a local church hall, then escort them home afterwards. They were placed in this work by the local Volunteer Bureau. They are helped by 19 year old Julia, a friend who is unemployed.

B.

Jack, Roger and Lynda spend 2 mornings a week approaching organisations about jobs for young people who complete 12 months in a youth training scheme run by a charitable trust. Jack and Roger were placed in this when the Trust approached REACH (Retired Executive Action Clearing House). Lynda, who is 30, came into contact through her husband who is one of the charity's trustees.

C.

George, 36, an unemployed electrician has fitted a special wall plug for a reading lamp for Susan (45) who is handicapped and housebound. She addresses envelopes for Andrew, Secretary of the school PTA, and Andrew helped fit double glazing for Jenny who teaches guitar to the daughter of Angela who . . .

Each of these examples describes different alternatives to employment. **A** and **B** are traditionally known as 'voluntary work'. **C** is also voluntary, but not quite the same as there is an exchange of time and talents between members of the community. Such schemes are known variously as *networks, worknets, skill exchanges, job swaps* or *community help.*

Voluntary work

It is only a few years since the term 'voluntary work' often implied amateur do-gooders more concerned with their own interests than those of the people they were helping. Now this has changed because:

- with the colossal reduction in regular work opportunities there has been an explosion in voluntary activities;

- today people from every walk of life and from different backgrounds are involved in voluntary activities;

- the level of professionalism in most of these activities is increasing—possibly because the quality, experience, and expertise of people who are involved is so much wider, and groups are learning rapidly from one another;

- although many people had strong political views against voluntary work a few years ago, now many more believe it can be useful. They understand that voluntary workers can find gaps in the statutory services and respond to them much more quickly than officials can. An example is the 'Dial-a-Ride' service in Leicester and Sheffield, described later. People now appreciate that communities get more self-respect from doing things for themselves than having other people do things for them.

Voluntary work does not include community work ordered by courts or organised by people paid under an MSC scheme (though there may be a mixture of voluntary workers and paid people in the same scheme). The old picture of flowery hatted ladies in soup kitchens (see cartoon) has certainly changed. Voluntary workers include people like first aid and mountain rescue teams, and organisers of the community sports, music, art or flower festivals.

Funds

Even with all the recent cuts in public expenditure, the

Government still allocates money for 'Opportunities for Volunteering'. This provides grants to increase the opportunities for voluntary work in health and social services. If you want to know more about these grants, you can find out from

The National Council of Voluntary Organisations,
26 Bedford Square, London WC1B 3AU.
Tel. 01-636 4066

Other groups launch their own fund-raising activities, or you can approach registered charities.

Getting in touch

The range, scope and details of voluntary organisations are too vast to list here. There are literally tens of thousands of groups. Some are large and permanent, such as Dr. Barnado's Homes, Age Concern, MENCAP, and MIND. Others are set up for a specific event, such as a street party or festival. You can find out what opportunities there are from local church officials, your local Council for Voluntary Services, Volunteer Bureau, Citizens Advice Bureau or Civic Information Services (usually situated in the Public Library). Some cities publish a directory. Just some examples of the types of community scheme now operating are as follows:

Networks/Skills exchanges

What are they?

The more developed schemes, such as in Liverpool, are a whole way of working without money, creating work which may or may not have been there before, or tackling a backlog of work in the community in exchange for something else of economic, creative or social value. Even modest schemes achieve quite a lot of these objectives.

Who starts them?

Some are started by adult education workers or student groups within an Adult Education Centre. Others are initiated in Unemployment 'Drop-In' centres or by church workers, paid or volunteers.

Who runs them?

Once it has been started, much of the work is done by the members. Manning the telephone, maintaining records of jobs done and putting up 'Available' or 'Wanted' cards daily are some of the jobs which can be exchanged.

Notice the difference between this and the local radio 'phone-in' swaps. Often no direct swap is possible because the person needing something has nothing relevant to offer to the person who has it, but the *Network* principle of exchanges means people are doing things for each other.

How is the work valued?

It isn't! There is no question of trying to exchange the same value in services or time. All members are expected to contribute something other than money—skills, services, knowledge, or just time to help run the scheme. If the work was valued, there could be implications for DHSS payments or Income Tax.

Who can join?

Membership is usually open to anybody in the community, on the principle that everybody has something to offer whether employed or not, infirm, old or young, of any social class or group, professional or unskilled, individual or group. A membership card is often used, and this is renewed annually.

What is needed and who pays for it?

A roof over your head, desk, chair, telephone and stationery, a large notice-board with cards and pins, plus a situation where the facility is visible, such as the entrance to a well used hall or on a busy street. Where projects have been started by adult education workers, an office or facilities within their centre has been used. Others have received help from Urban Aid funds through their Local Authority. Start-up funds for initial efforts to advertise and test out local interest have come from churches, residents' associations, and charities.

Protection!

You must take one or two basic precautions, and make these clear to all members:

- It is best to avoid work normally done by skilled artisans (plumbing, electrical wiring, brickwork, etc.), unless you are absolutely satisfied that the person doing the job is qualified and experienced. Helping an elderly person or single parent by repapering and painting the kitchen is one thing—fitting new gas pipes or an electrical socket is quite another!

- You must allocate the first funds to taking out appropriate insurance for *public liability*, in case of any damage to property or person by a member. (One reason for having formal membership, not general openness to anyone who pops in, is to assure both the insurance company and the members that you have vetting and control.) An accident policy covering a person doing any work is also beneficial and usually inexpensive. If you extend into other activities, e.g. social, make sure your insurance covers these too.

Potential

Networks such as Liverpool and a local Sheffield group have developed to the stage where they have one or more paid community workers helping on the scheme, paid for by the Local Authority or Manpower Services Commission. Some have a number of community-based groups which are in touch with each other. This makes them large enough to have joint social activities or coach trips, negotiate special rates for leisure activities or purchasing goods, develop educational facilities for members and their families, produce a newsletter, collect statistics about exchanges, and stimulate new groups in districts not already covered.

Objections

- Won't Trade Unions object?
- How will local tradesmen view these activities?

In Merseyside the Unions were consulted when the scheme began and raised no objection, and one regional office considered starting its own scheme for members. The main fears are of people being exploited by giving work they could be paid for. But experience in Sheffield and Merseyside shows that the type of person most likely to try to exploit others is put off because the work is reciprocal, and the records show up a scrounger. Finally, any member has the right to say 'No' to a job if they feel they are being used.

As for tradesmen, three points are worth making:

1. Much of the work would not otherwise be done at all, as people could not afford it, or would try to do it themselves. The Network would not tackle large contracts.

2. Small building firms are busiest and dislike putting artisans on to very small jobs, because they are less profitable than larger jobs, like building an extension.

3. Local traders benefit by purchase of materials for odd jobs which people could not otherwise afford to have done.

In practice, there has not been exploitation. Most schemes actually find more people offer services than use them.

Education

People's attitudes need changing:

- some people won't believe they have anything to offer;
- some people believe anything done for them free of charge is 'charity'. Older people especially worry that any voluntary work done for them might make officials think they cannot cope, and that then they will be institutionalised.

An elderly man living alone in Sheffield had repairs done by the Council which left his home in 'a hell of a mess'. The local Skills Exchange offered to help clean up. He refused and paid for outside help which he could ill afford. His reason: 'I don't want charity'.

Directory of Community Resources

If there is no such Directory in your city or area, why not set the ball rolling? In Sheffield, the Manpower Services Commission funded two people to research this by sending out questionnaires and co-ordinating the replies for publication. One did the compiling and the other typed it. The City Council sponsored the project, and the finished product has 300 pages, with 1000 entries in 24 sections. It lists:

- all community and voluntary groups in the city;
- accommodation for elderly, children, mentally and physically handicapped;
- advice centres, legal information and consumer advice centres;
- care for the elderly;
- youth and community centres;
- help for the disabled;
- support for families and children;
- organisations for ethnic minorities;
- resources and media;

- and much more besides!

The first 500 copies sold out in the first month at £5 each. It created 2 jobs to compile it, and will presumably need one to keep it up to date.

Dial-a-Ride

Established voluntary groups in Leicester and Sheffield have received grants through the Local Authority from Urban Aid to purchase one or two vehicles which have been specially adapted to take wheel chairs and cope with the disabled. Volunteers or Community Programme workers drive the vehicles, for which the hirers pay expenses on a mileage basis.

The service arose because drivers of many conventional hire car or taxi firms would not take people who could not get themselves in and out of the car. The Dial-a-Ride vehicles have lift platforms and ramps for rear entry, and a minibus can take groups out together, including 2 passengers in wheel chairs. Individuals and organisations register as members of the scheme, for insurance purposes, and so that drivers are sure the people concerned are genuinely incapacitated.

Charity Information Service

This service was set up in South Yorkshire for grant givers and grant seekers. It means a group looking for funds can apply to charities concerned with *their* needs, rather than wasting time writing off to charities who have other concerns.

This is another project funded by the Manpower Services Commission, but volunteers have been used to cope because the work has grown so much.

You can get more information from

The South Yorks. Charity Information Service, 40 Trippett Lane, Sheffield S1 4EL. Phone (0742) 731765.

Setting up such a service in your area could be useful to other voluntary organisations.

Voluntary projects programme

The pamphlet shown in the picture on the opposite page explains a great deal about this programme which is funded by the Manpower

Services Commission. This is included here because it is a mixture of full-time workers organising volunteers in their own neighbourhood. The scheme requires a sponsor, which in the example shown is a parish church. The funds for the full-time workers as well as the travel expenses shown on the pamphlet are all provided by the MSC.

You can obtain more details on the conditions and rules for this programme and others from your local MSC office.

Like to improve your job prospects by doing something constructive while brushing up existing skills or learning new ones?

VPP is designed to increase the self-confidence and motivation of unemployed people; to enhance their work skills and improve their prospects of moving into employment or formal education or training. Projects include adult education classes in social skills, literacy, numeracy and computing; others involve local community and voluntary activities such as environmental work or furniture renovation; and some help people prepare for self-employment.

Who is eligible?

1. To participate
Anyone unemployed aged between 16 and State pension age, whether receiving benefits or not, who is willing to give a number of hours or days a week.

2. To sponsor projects
Any organisation or group of individuals: for example, local authorities, private companies, voluntary bodies, charities.

Financial help

Participation is voluntary and does not affect entitlement to unemployment or supplementary benefits, whether you work for a few hours or a full five-day week. Although participants are unpaid, those undertaking work of community benefit may receive travelling expenses up to £5 a week.

Financial help is given to sponsors up to a maximum of £75,000 for any single project to fund its employees and approved running costs.

Sponsors wishing to provide meals to VPP workers on community work projects may be reimbursed up to 50 per cent of the approved costs of providing the meals, up to 50p per meal.

Contact
Your local Jobcentre. Sponsors should contact their nearest Community Programme Area Office (see page 36).

DHSS Implications

If you are doing voluntary work while receiving social security or unemployment benefits, it need not affect your benefits. There is a useful DHSS pamphlet called *Voluntary Work and Social Security Benefits*, N1 240, which explains all this.

The general principle is that your benefits are not affected as long as the voluntary work does not stop you being available for a job or interview, that you could go at 24 hours notice, and you are not being paid more than £2 per day plus reasonable expenses.

The pamphlet is useful for up-to-date information on which

payments and benefits (such as travel, N.I. contribution and meals) are and are not taken into account when working out how much you could earn. There is also a 30-hour rule which operates if you are doing 'paid voluntary work' (that is time is given freely, but you are paid expenses and a little pocket money), unless you are doing certain jobs such as being on the crew of a life-boat or a part-time fireman.

Unfortunately, although many of these rules are clear, there is disagreement within the DHSS as to what constitutes voluntary work in schemes which reciprocate services without money changing hands. For example, the DHSS in Liverpool and most parts of Sheffield accept the Skills Exchange scheme as voluntary work (after all it is rarely more than half a day a week), but in some areas DHSS officers have warned that benefits will not be paid to participants in the scheme, thus killing it at birth. It is sometimes useful to be able to quote a precedent, but it cuts no ice with some officials. There is a right of appeal to a local tribunal and it's worth clearing it up before starting.

Voluntary and community schemes—MSC

The names, scope and allowances paid under these schemes vary from time to time, so I shall not include all the details here as so far few of them have remained unchanged for more than 2–3 years. From time to time, some are the subject of political debate and dispute. Others are used by voluntary agencies, with a good deal of misgiving about certain aspects of them. But the agencies cannot take too rigid a stand, or they would deprive those most in need. Governments might put less strain on the voluntary sector's goodwill if they consulted more before setting the rules!

Useful publications on volunteering are:

1. *Government Grants—A Guide for Voluntary Organisations.* (Bedford Square Press) £3.95.
2. *A Matter of Choice: Unemployed Volunteering and Volunteer Bureaux* by Kevin Ford. £3 (inc post).

Obtainable from Project VBX, Unit 15, Arches Industrial Estate, Spoon End, Coventry CV1 3JQ.

⑥ Activity for Purpose and Pleasure

In this chapter I shall talk about *what can be done* and *where to start,* including such activities as

community cafés and
rights and advice centres.

These activities are valuable to the community in general, and can provide an operating base and give viability to an active group.

I shall then discuss other activities and facilities which provide opportunities for groups or individuals, including a collective approach to:

job finding
retraining planning
job creation
consultancy
self-development
adult education

I shall also discuss various ways in which people have organised themselves for community care and a variety of other activities.

Self-help is a growing trend. People are disillusioned with the failure of institutions to fulfil their hopes. Increasingly they are rejecting dependency on professionals and authorities.

First I shall repeat two principles:

- work does not necessarily mean a paid job—although I hope it will be this for some people involved;

- I do not put 'work' and 'leisure' into two separate compartments.

Leisure time is really *choosing time:* what we choose to do—manual work, reading, sport—is more truly leisure than activity directed by other people. Leisure is not just the absence of work. And it is not the same as *recreation*—activities which 're-create' us as whole people. Time off from paid employment, often called 'leisure time' is often spent on work in the home, with voluntary organisations or in political activity.

We would get more out of life if we did not feel that work, leisure and recreation were all separate activities.

I do not mean 'get on and do something and don't worry about being paid'. I do mean that finding a purpose to our lives may not have a lot to do with money. If we truly believe that what we are doing is *worthwhile*—for a community or for our own development—and that we *enjoy* doing it, then we should not feel guilty that we are not doing what society calls a 'proper job'. The sort of activities I am thinking of might be taking a part-time or full-time study course, helping out on day trips for children or elderly folk, or challenging a decision to close down the only Job Centre in your vicinity.

What to do?

It would be easy to list lots of different suggestions and activities and say 'Pick one or think up something of your own'. But other publications do this.

You might like to get hold of *Church Action with the Unemployed* which outlines about 100 schemes, although 75 per cent depend on MSC funding. You can get this from

146 Queen Victoria Street, London EC4V 4BY. Tel. 01 236 8430

Another worthwhile publication is *Action with the Unemployed.* You can get this from

British Unemployment Resource Network, 318 Summer Lane, Birmingham B19 3RL.

If you have bothered to read this far, you probably already wanted to get something going before you picked up this book.

I have already said that you should

- think clearly what you are trying to do;
- become active and visible as soon as possible, so people involved don't lose heart;
- get known in the community.

If you have already decided that what you want is simply to find a way to start a business, then what comes next is probably not for you—so move on.

If you want to create a centre where people in your area can get together to some purpose, perhaps to generate some jobs and create a 'presence'—then read on.

Where to start—basics

You may have an ideal pattern in your mind of how you want your project to go, but you very often have to start in a small way. However, I can think of two activities which get people active and highly visible fairly quickly, and which are reasonably cheap to set up, if you have a roof over your head. They can be staffed by different people at different times, you don't need one person to do a full week.

Rights and Advice centre

This mainly requires a room, a desk and a few chairs, and a telephone. It also needs people with the drive to get brochures and pamphlets from a variety of sources such as the DHSS, Local Authority's Housing or Consumer Protection Department, or Employment Offices, and to find out what they don't know about benefits, etc. Some centres specialise in advice for the elderly. Others are more general.

People often use these centres because they don't want to make a direct approach themselves. They may fear officials, or worry that asking questions might make them less likely to be successful, e.g. with the DHSS. So they like to know where they stand first.

These centres seem to have some things in common:

- Some manage to obtain a small grant from their local

authority, or have people on placement from an MSC programme. Many are run by volunteers, who can become incredibly knowledgeable and dependable. A newcomer can receive help and training either from an experienced person in another centre, or from a Citizens Advice Bureau.

- A frequent problem for these centres is that once volunteers know what they are doing and are really useful, they are snapped up by agencies that can pay a salary. So this could be a way into a job for someone good at this type of work. The really important thing is that a lot of people get experience in battling for benefits or grants, and gain self-confidence in their ability to find out what they don't know.

- Such a centre involves people in serving one another. Those who run them are not dependent on others while working there, and they gain self-confidence and independence, which will stand them in good stead when they move on, regardless of what they do next.

Another idea, and one which is often run alongside a Rights and Advice centre, is a

Community café
This sort of café is also an activity with a purpose. It fulfils a need, because almost everybody wants a hot or cold drink some time in the day. In their organisation and in what they offer, community cafés vary enormously.

Some are co-operatives (registered or unregistered), with members working maybe full-time or one day a week, or even less. Frequently their prices are decided on so as to give each person involved an income at least equivalent to the statutory minimum wage.

Others operate on a 'trust' basis. Users bring in prepared dishes, on a rota basis, and are paid just enough to cover ingredients and cooking costs. This keeps prices to the minimum, and is particularly helpful if most of the customers are unemployed. It is unnecessary if they are not. Some even operate on a 'help yourself' basis, where customers leave their cash in a box in exchange for what they take.

A café can give people a chance to sample a wider range of foods than they might have tried otherwise. For example, some cafés serve vegetarian dishes.

So it is important to decide on your objectives before you start. If you want to provide a service to the community at large and create some jobs in the process, then a café serving a range of attractive and wholesome food at reasonable prices is appropriate— especially if there is no such service already available nearby or centrally.

If your aim is a mutual service for people on low incomes, and/or a warm place where people can bring their families or older people in cold weather to save on heating bills at home, and get a meal they can afford, this will affect what you cook and how it is priced.

If your café is also to be educational, possibly with cookery classes, again this needs to be stated and thought out. You must know who you are aiming at.

A café can be a focal, meeting and information point for a community, and a place for leaving messages, selling home-made goods, putting up posters, or cards for 'sales and wants'.

Rural community café

An imaginative community café has been set up in St Austell in Cornwall. It is known as The Filling Station, and has become a focal point for people on low incomes. It co-ordinates all the groups in the area interested in 'alternative economy' activities, such as organically-grown vegetables and recycling waste. It is also a centre for entertainment groups of all sorts.

The Filling Station is a registered co-operative and part of a larger network—CADURN, the Cornwall and Devon Unemployment Resources Network, which was formed in 1983 to provide a support system for people in isolated places where unemployment is high (25 per cent in Falmouth). Both CADURN and The Filling Station have policies of avoiding grants with their attached strings.

Offices and workshops

A feature of many centres is office or workshop space, for a variety of purposes.

- Some provide facilities to enable the unemployed to 'keep their hand in', so that if jobs become available they will be able to take them up. Facilities often include typewriters and other office equipment, sewing machines, small lathes and woodwork tools with work benches. Unfortunately those I have seen bear little relation to local industries, and often there is no real prospect of a job for most of those who attend.

- Some provide community groups with a place to produce typed or duplicated matter. Individuals can use the workshops for making items they would not be able to buy, or to make either without the right tools, space and work benches. So tool libraries have also become a feature. (See the Brunswick Centre Poster opposite.) Users have to provide their own wood or other materials, and those with skills are on hand to advise and assist those less able.

Some workshops, such as IMPASSE in Middlesbrough, have obtained grants from the MSC to pay an instructor in each of the skill areas available—woodwork, photography, printing, video work and so on. But beware! A privileged group of employed instructors in a community of unemployed people must create an inner group. To some extent it destroys the principle of mutual support, giving and receiving on an equal footing. It also means, inevitably, that people are less inclined to assist voluntarily. It seems to me important that CADURN (referred to above) have rejected this option. It is almost certainly because, although they have different political views, they have hammered out their objectives collectively. Once you become dependent on outside funding for regular income, it's very difficult to lose it!

Job search

A centre for the unemployed can provide a good roof under which to start various collaborative approaches to

finding a job, exploring retraining opportunities, setting up new enterprises (individually, in partnerships or co-operatives), support services and consultancies for small businesses and voluntary organisations.

If you set about this in a methodical and businesslike way, you could well attract assistance from banks or other organisations, by way of staff members being attached to deal with the administration, or funding from a local authority or county council.

I shall describe a whole range of activities, but it is probably best to start with a more limited range. Experience shows that such

LOPHAM STREET COMMUNITY WORKSHOP Tel. 20863

we offer you basic......
"tools"
you are all welcome
the workshop is free of charge

open

9am

SPACE, MATERIALS AND PLANS TO MAKE FURNITURE, TOYS, EQUIPMENT, CLOTHES, FOR YOU, YOUR FAMILY AND FRIENDS OR FOR SALE.
WE CAN DO YOUR PRINTING AT A REASONABLE RATE, OR TEACH YOU TO USE THE MACHINES. WE CAN HELP WITH IDEAS, DESIGN, AND KNOW-HOW

daily

4pm

photograph room now
open

BRUNSWICK centre,

activities are more likely to succeed when they come from within the community and are properly prepared and thought through, than when brought in from outside or left to individuals to struggle with on their own.

The sketch below shows the sorts of things a job search centre might try to do:

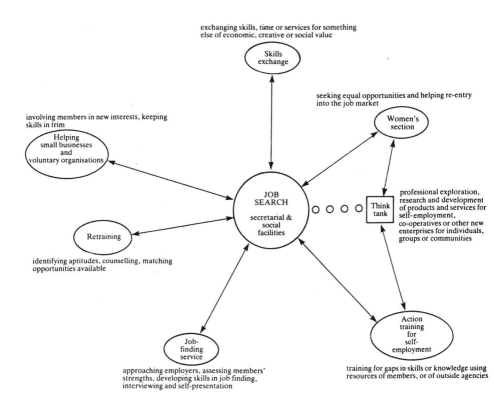

Some local authorities have made it their business to learn how to obtain money from the European Social Fund (ESF). So if you can make a proposal to them in the first place, indicating where they can recover the funding they might give you, it can only help your cause. In addition to training and retraining schemes proper, the ESF can finance studies and *pilot schemes* 'which are innovative in nature and help to guide the fund in its main area of intervention'.

Sources

Some of the activities described here in outline have been tried in a scheme in Birmingham known as 'Job Change', a point venture between the Birmingham Settlement and the City of Birmingham Polytechnic. Guy Dauncey describes this in some detail in *Nice Work If You Can Get It**. Other ideas come from experiences with self-help groups of unemployed people and from a management education project in 'self-development' which we refer to later.

Job finding

Most job seeking is done by individuals. Most letters of application are written in answer to an advert or notice in a job centre.

The alternative, which some groups do very successfully, is to take the initiative. In other words, don't wait for employers to have a vacancy—unite to persuade them that when they do have a job going it will be to their own benefit to contact your group first. The benefits to them include savings in advertising costs, time saving on recruitment, a better chance to fit a round peg into a round hole, even the possibility of 'swapping' somebody who has turned out not to have the aptitudes needed.

The important thing here is the joint approach, and the effort of the unemployed members using skilled help to assess their personal strengths and likely usefulness to a possible employer, or to society. This is important in re-establishing self-esteem and confidence for an interview. In addition it harnesses the skills and experience of members in helping one another to write effective applications and produce curriculum vitae, in interview training and self-presentation, and in keeping a register of appropriate skills and experience.

Selling the goodies

Meanwhile, other people with contacts and selling experience are out visiting potential employers—no easy task! Here are some lessons learned the hard way:

Phoning for an appointment is seldom effective. Usually people

---

* Published by NEC.

want to know why you want to see them, and when you tell them they don't want to see you.

Writing seldom produces any reply.

Writing and enclosing an addressed return postcard for the receiver to post back confirming an appointment produces a few more replies than just writing, but hardly justifies the effort.

The most effective way is to write to say that you are coming to see the person concerned at a particular time and date. This produces about a one in three chance of an interview—higher than any other method!

An important aid to this success is writing to a known name in the organisation you are going to—not just to 'The Personnel Manager', or similar title. It pays to take time and effort to find out. Sometimes members of your group may know. Otherwise a phone call to the company switchboard can produce the name. If a straightforward direct question is not answered, try a more subtle indirect approach.

What do you say to them?
There are two points worth making to the person you see, to encourage them to consider your members first when recruiting:

1. The effort and energy your members put into the project to find a job is a reflection on their willingness to get down to a job of work. They are not getting paid for this. How much more effort will they put in for an employer who is able to offer a wage!

2. Any member the employer takes on is an ambassador for your group, because you want him to come back to you again when he has another vacancy. If you can assure the employer of the quality of your product, that you can save him time and money advertising and provide the right person for the job, then the chances are that your group will get a trial next time a vacancy occurs. Mind you, if your choice lets you down, that will be the end of it, so you must make sure your homework and preparation are up to scratch!

Other points

- Keep a card index of all calls made and what happened for each company, and the name of the person seen.

- If you get one or two successful appointments, tell other companies when you visit them which company has tried it and who to refer to.

- Have every member of your group on the look-out to feed in information or news about anybody taking on staff.

Training, retraining and development

One spin-off of personal assessment is that members identify aptitudes and interests which can be a guide towards an appropriate retraining programme. Anyone who has never had a grant for further education may be better off thinking about retraining than endlessly applying for jobs in their old trade. Adult careers advisers in the local Careers Service can be helpful in getting people thinking along these lines, to identify the appropriate course to attend.

Self-development

Funds can be obtained from the MSC by a credible group to fund an adult education or training consultant to run what are known as 'self-development' or 'action-learning' groups, especially if they are likely to lead to some members setting up in business on their own. Sometimes such programmes qualify participants for an allowance while attending, and these can run up to 26 weeks. There are three important principles on which such programmes are based:

- they concentrate on the *real* issues and needs of the participants—so there is no case study teaching, and no academic lectures;

- the learners direct activities—not the trainers. The trainers do not make assumptions about what the participants need. They are there to help them decide what they need, and to show them what resources there are and how best to use them;

- probably the people most likely to be able to help members of these groups are the other members of the group. For this really to work, there must be a level of openness and trust which has to be worked at.

A typical self-development programme looks like this:

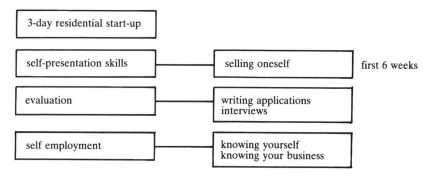

Following this, participants work in groups of six, continuously raising issues, evaluating, challenging and supporting one another, taking responsibility for their own actions and reporting back to each other. It is important to be able to keep confidences in order to trust. Participants may meet weekly in the meantime, setting out to get something planned or started.

Experience has shown that this is by far the most effective way of assisting potential entrepreneurs. Traditional management courses, or even polytechnic courses, are of some value, *but*

- few of the staff have experience of small business themselves,
- the courses are too generalised for the day to day rough and tumble of the 'one man band'.

In self-development programmes the learning material comes from each person's own experiences of trying to get funds, finding premises or customers, trying to decide how to advertise to best effect on a limited budget, or how to increase or improve stock without borrowing more money.

This does not mean that outside expertise cannot be brought in if necessary. But the participants themselves decide who to invite and how they can help.

Support services

The unemployed have knowledge and skills which could be used by small businesses or voluntary organisations. The success of organisations like REACH (Retired Executives Action Clearing House) and volunteer bureaux around the country shows that different types of organisations are often pleased to have help—sometimes paid for, sometimes paying only expenses. The important benefit to the unemployed person is that acting as a consultant/adviser or helper keeps up morale and gives a feeling of being wanted and useful. It also gives an interest in life and keeps skills in trim.

The Skills Exchange activity described in Chapter 5 also fits in with this activity.

Think tank

Job-finding and retraining programmes are very valuable, but there is a real need to create new jobs. This is not easy.

Nevertheless, people do come up with new ideas for products and services. This group's task would be to explore the development of such products or ideas, possibly locating funds for feasibility studies or market research. Membership of the group would include people with experience in design, production, marketing and finance skills. This 'think tank' would not just advise, it would work closely with would-be entrepreneurs.

•

All the activities listed above under 'job search' are purposeful and creative, and many unemployed people have found them worthwhile. They have often been the road back to employed, paid work. For some people, the chance to work through an idea for self-employment leads to a new career. Others are saved a lot of heartache and debt by finding that their business idea has a major flaw. Some people find as long as they have enough to live on, their lives can be creative, useful and extremely satisfying, helping other unemployed people, or acting as advisers to small businesses, the self-employed or a voluntary organisation. This is often the case for people who have to take redundancy or early retirement, aged 50 or over, whose experience and knowledge is invaluable to others.

Administration

It may seem to contradict what I said in the earlier chapters about self-reliance, to suggest having an administrator on secondment from a bank or company. But the amount of administrative work in a large project, and the size of funds involved, could be too much for one volunteer. Dividing the admin jobs between volunteers could be disruptive and make communication very difficult. An administrator from a bank or company could also help to reassure those likely to provide funding that the administration is on a sound footing. The trustees or management council—the unemployed members' representatives—would still retain control and provide signatories for cheques or other documents.

Adult education classes

Most adult education is not aimed at gaining qualifications. It is for the sheer enjoyment of learning and the acquisition of new knowledge, or to acquire or improve a skill such as DIY, art or embroidery. You can learn skills like computer programming with a view to employment later, but if you really want a new skill for a job, you should think of retraining and taking a full-time course.

Some people use adult education if they are not sure if they could cope with something more advanced, to see how they get on before going further.

In many places now, especially in centres for the unemployed, the choice of subjects is decided by the needs of the people who want to attend, and the local authority provides funds and tutors. Of course, if you have the facilities there is nothing to stop you recruiting a volunteer to train, lecture or instruct.

Classes can lead to or spring from other activities in the centre. I have already mentioned cookery classes as a by-product of a community café. Other people have started a marketing co-operative to sell the products of art, handicraft, needlework, dressmaking, needlework, embroidery or other classes. But this is not always easy!

Ill-feeling arose in an informal co-operative of people attending adult education classes when it became clear that out of 50–60 people attending classes, only about a dozen were prepared to put time into the selling side.

The dispute was eventually resolved by a third party outsider who, after questioning those involved, pointed out that some people were there primarily for their own education, not for profit. Others were quite interested in selling the odd item, but those most interested in the co-op saw it as an additional source of income.

The dispute was resolved by separating the selling from the education, with the keen group doing the selling. All items were on 'sale or return', and the seller took 20 per cent of the selling price for overheads.

The people who organized this project came under further fire from the local Co-operative Development Agency officer who insisted that they stopped calling themselves a co-operative because they weren't registered. They were also criticised by the Education Department who didn't like a commercial activity operating on the back of adult education. So before you start on such an activity, it is just as well to make sure it won't upset anybody.

•

Your local adult education office will put you in touch with various sources of materials. You can also get a useful set of brochures from the **Open University** by writing to:

The Learning Materials Service Office, Ref CG 44,
The Open University,
PO Box 188,
Milton Keynes MK7 6DH

The Open University brochure is called *Community Education Courses and Packs* and is updated each year. It includes courses on health, retirement, various aspects of pregnancy, birth, and child-rearing from infancy to teenage, including pre-school playgroups; caring for the elderly, matters affecting family life including family abuse and legal matters, healthy eating, energy saving, work and racism. All in all a fairly comprehensive selection spread across most sectors of the community.

It also has a useful pack called *The Unemployment Project,* to help the unemployed

- tackle immediate practical problems;
- assess their interests, achievements, skills and potential;
- explore questions for the future and draw up action plans.

There are 8 themes in the pack, each contained within a 4-page topic leaflet.

•

The **National Extension College** also has some useful community education material, including:

1. *Absolute musts*
   Community Start Up
   Self-Help Learning Groups

2. *Unemployment and work*
   The New Unemployment Handbook updated 1986
   Nice Work If You Can Get It
   Your Work in Your Hands

3. *Small businesses*
   Be Your Own Boss—Starter Kit updated 1986
   Be Your Own Boss—Growth Kit updated booklet 1986
   Languages for Business—an information pack for people running small businesses in most Asian languages and Chinese

4. *Directories*
   Second Chances 86/87
   Open Tech Directory

5. *Parent education*
   The Parent Book

6. *Computing and wordprocessing courses*
   15 Hour Wordprocessing—
      VIEW
      Wordwise and Wordwise Plus
      Amstrad
      Wordstar
      Practical Exercises
   All Fingers Go
   Typing Tester
   Data and Word Processing

7. *Basic education and study skills*
   Study skills series
      Grammar
      How to Improve Your Handwriting
      How to Study Effectively
      How to Use Your Dictionary
      How to Write Essays
      Learning to Study
      Report Writing
      Studying
      Writing
      Writing Letters

Community care

There are a number of imaginative schemes around the country set up to look after the elderly, handicapped, long-term hospitalised, the housebound or people living alone. Some are run entirely by volunteers. Others are partially funded by the MSC under the Community Programme, Opportunities for Volunteering, or the Voluntary Projects Programme. (There is a difference between these last two!)

In one scheme at a mining village in South Yorkshire, a volunteer group known as 'Voltage' has for several years run a rota for neighbourhood help and care, to fill the gaps which the usual professional services could not hope to fill.

One lady organised a tea to follow the funeral of an 85 year old man whose 84 year old wife was too frail to do anything about it.

Another spent time each week helping out a young woman with new twins. The mother found it hard to cope at first, having no previous experience with babies.

Another was contacted by a local doctor late one night, and spent the night sitting at the bedside of someone who had had a stroke, until he could be admitted to hospital the next morning.

Such schemes need the co-operation of local doctors, social workers and home helps—not always an easy matter.

In a London inner city district, two regular volunteers run what amounts to a drop-in centre for the elderly. It provides a point of contact and a place to keep warm cheaply. Once a week older members of the community in long-stay hospitals are brought to meet others, to keep in touch and reduce their sense of isolation. There are packs of cards and papers and magazines, and a kitchen nearby so tea or coffee can be served.

First get your facts straight – a case study

The vicar of a parish in Yorkshire was concerned

- for the large numbers of unemployed quoted in the local press, and the lack of facilities for them;
- with the large church and church hall which were used very little by the ageing and dwindling congregation.

He and a volunteer from his congregation (a lady who had been made redundant) set about thinking how they could assist the unemployed. They decided firstly to talk to local social workers and discovered two important facts:

- the immediate church neighbourhood did not contain as many unemployed as they expected;

- there was an unusually large number of elderly and disabled people, and people living alone in the area, with very little provision for them.

They obtained agreement from the MSC to use the Community Programme, but under a larger scheme for which the managing agents were the Local Council for Voluntary Services. As sponsors, the church would choose their own workers, but their administration and pay would be the responsibility of the managing agents.

The first appointment was the lady worker as supervisor. Next, CP (Community Programme) workers were taken on to cook and deliver hot meals to the elderly, disabled or people living alone who did not qualify for 'Meals on Wheels', and to back up these with an hour's talking and listening. Arrangements were also made to tape church services for those who liked them, but with no pressure on anyone to take them.

The Family Centre now employs 11 full- and part-time staff to service the community, going out to their houses and offering facilities and socially useful services in the centre. There is a catering officer and assistant, 5 'contact workers', including one with an inventive flair specialising in aids for disabled people, 2 handymen/gardeners and a social/activity co-ordinator. There is a regular parent/toddler group, a lunch club 2 days a week with entertainment, and a fortnightly special lunch for pensioners only. It is open daily from 10.30 a.m. for coffee.

The centre has succeeded in keeping up contacts with a wide cross-section of the community:

- working people, including bank staff and shopkeepers, call in for lunch one day a week;

- the local comprehensive school has 6th formers assisting in the kitchen, waiting at tables and helping with the toddler group; the drama society and school orchestra entertain after lunch, woodwork classes make walking sticks or aids for the handicapped; some youngsters work in houses or dig gardens;

- nurses from a nearby group general practice call in regularly for referral;

- local police keep contact workers informed of elderly people with problems or potentially at risk;

- local authority health visitors or home helps call for contact workers to assist if they feel somebody should be kept a closer eye on;

- hospital welfare officers (a) advise of patients discharged, and (b) send small groups of long-stay geriatrics to a lunch club weekly.

About 150 people are visited regularly. About 20 come in by social services minibus weekly, and about 40–50 attend the community lunches.

•

Finance

Staff wages and administration are handled by the CVS who are managing agents. The church, as sponsor, currently receives a grant from the MSC of £125 per head annually for overheads (light, heat, maintenance). Grants are also received from other organisations, such as Age Concern, and donations of equipment from commercial companies.

Policy and Conclusions

An important feature of this project, with useful lessons, is the care taken in the early stages to make sure that the decisions are based on sound information and carefully prepared.

- It would have been easy to assume that unemployment problems were the same as elsewhere in the city, and to plan activities exclusively for such people. Careful questioning, and a policy of ensuring that people were helping each other, gave a different emphasis to the project and ensured that the *real* problems were tackled.

- Great care was taken to liaise with the Local Authority and Social Services to ensure that home helps and social workers would not feel threatened, and that the scheme would not be seen as a cheap substitute. Copies of job descriptions were obtained, and job titles and descriptions in the project were designed not to overlap with home helps. So initial suspicions and reservations were overcome, and there is now full co-operation and information. Officials often call on the centre for emergency help until the official wheels can turn into action.

- The patron, supervisor and staff stress the need for entertainment, and for activities to be creative and artistic. Bingo is virtually banned! 'There is more to old people than spots before the eyes,' as the vicar put it. There is a real concern to keep out 'cabbage' type activities, and to feed in those which are life enhancing. Long-term they foresee a more developed programme of adult education for the elderly.

- The frequent house visiting has thrown up an awareness of a large number of untenanted buildings in the area. They are trying to work out how to use this information, as these deprive the area of trade and facilities, and generally impoverish the community.

•

A spin-off for the sponsor has been a return to the church by some residents. Although he insists that this was not the original purpose of the exercise, it is a result of feedback from the wider community which sees the church no longer only interested in opening its doors on Sunday and forgetting them for the rest of the week.

Most important—the members of the scheme are in daily contact with the rest of the community, either through home visiting or the community visiting the centre. There is a mutuality of service, so each has an opportunity to find a purpose in serving others who are in deprived circumstances not of their own making.

The self-respect and confidence gained by the unemployed workers in particular has resulted in several who were out of work for more than a year finding better paid permanent work within 3 months of starting with the project. Those who don't, receive counselling and help to develop new skills or take retraining.

A 'support group' of local doctors, social workers and others reviews the progress and objectives of the scheme quarterly, with the patron. It would complete the picture if the CP workers or representatives were involved in this exercise as well.

Community care – an umbrella

With the government laying increased stress on the support the voluntary sector can give in the community, the National Council of Voluntary Organisations has set up a 'Community Care Project' to look at problems faced by such activities in the UK. Often, projects which start off with realistic objectives find themselves overloaded by increased demands by the DHSS for their help, but with their funds either reduced or under threat, e.g. from rate-capping. Initially, the project has a 3-year life span, from 1985. It is based at

Community Care Project,
NCVO,
26 Bedford Square,
London WC1B 3HU

Community health

This is another area where imaginative steps are being taken. Some are based on the growing belief that we can take much more responsibility for our own health than either the medical profession or the layman has ever before realised, or would like to acknowledge.

The result is a boom in dieting and healthy eating clubs, concerned at the effects that fast or 'junk' foods can have on our general health, and the possibility of them producing cancerous conditions. Many people now take increased exercise, including jogging, yoga, keep fit and nutrition classes. With these have come growth in alternative medicine and mutual help clubs for slimmers and smokers, for getting unhooked from drugs or tranquillisers, or for natural childbirth.

For community and ethnic groups there is a whole range of self-help activities, for every age from pre-birth and toddler, through to the elderly or bereaved. An Asian Women's project in Nottingham, for example, aims to help Asian women with language tuition, and advice on welfare benefit. Asian women visit wards in the University Hospital to make sure Asian patients' needs are understood and met if possible. So far their expenses have been met by grants from the Hospital trustees, and a 1984 grant from the Area Health Authority.

Details of community health activities can be obtained from

Community Health Initiatives Resource Unit,
NCVO,
26 Bedford Square,
London WC1B 3HU

Pressure Groups

Some groups have set out not to promote activities such as MSC schemes or create work, but to act as education and pressure groups. Some Centres for the Unemployed concentrate on these activities. In South Yorkshire each main centre of population has a 'Christian Unemployment Group' (CHUG) which holds public vigils, and family days for unemployment families, produces posters, challenges church job creation initiatives and MSC policies, runs seminars and issues information sheets on Youth Training Schemes, job creation, proposed changes in legislation affecting benefits or claimants rights, or raises petitions. Examples of their activities from the local press are shown below.

Conclusion

As we have seen, there is practically no limit to the areas and activities which could be brought into community contact or influence. The trend is increasing: health, work and community care are one example, and hospices for the dying, housing, food distribution and consumer protection. For a long time we have depended on 'them'—the government, the local authority, the medical profession, the company. But that dependence is changing. The realisation that a national government can no longer fully protect us from attack from outside has been accompanied by the realisation that we can trust ourselves more than 'them' in other areas. 'They' are not infallible.

Self-help in the community will probably be with us permanently. The popular view of the 1960s and early '70s—that self-help projects enable the government (of whatever persuasion) to escape its responsibilities, is now seen to be absurd on 2 counts:

- no government could possibly fill every gap; no government can respond quickly enough to new needs in a changing, dynamic situation, in the way that the voluntary sector can;
- people need to help one another; to deny this is to deny their integrity. We are born with a sense and a need to give and receive.

7 Working for a Profit – or at Least a Living!

It is arguable that everybody who works is aiming at some sort of profit, individually or collaboratively, for themselves or for others. In this chapter I shall address those who want to earn their own living, working either individually (possibly employing somebody else along the way), or collaboratively in a partnership or co-operative.

This is not intended to be a comprehensive guide to running your own business. There are already plenty of books for this, published by, among others, the NEC and the *Guardian* (see the list at the end of this chapter). I may repeat some of their conclusions, but I also hope to say some things they *don't* say.

Small business and unemployment

Promoting new small businesses as a major contribution to the relief of the unemployment problem is a continuing statement of faith in many quarters, not just in Westminster. I am all for making life reasonably straightforward for people starting their own enterprises, whether for themselves or the community. I am all for giving them support and professional help, whether paid for or free (though in my experience as a consultant, it's the expensive advice which gets acted on!).

But this has little to do with solving unemployment problems, except very marginally and in the very long term.

It takes nearly 10 years for new manufacturing industries to create new jobs in any significant numbers. (I don't mean opening a car factory—that is not a new industry!)

The number of small firms increased in the 1970s, yet employment in manufacturing industries declined.

New small firms can produce jobs, but they only *increase* jobs if births (or start-ups) exceed deaths. The rate of death for new firms runs at 40 per cent in their first year of operation, and at 90 per cent by the end of their fifth year! This failure rate has been constant for many years.

> In the 1970s a commendable programme for small firm development in Cleveland created less than 2,000 new jobs in wholly new firms surviving 11 years. But in one day in 1980, British Steel in Cleveland announced 3,000 job losses!

Some new enterprises have a better chance of success than others:

Low risk start-ups

The new start-ups least likely to fail are those created by high technology scientists who start up on their own in the type of industry in which they were formerly employed. Such people nearly all come from upper managerial grades in large firms, and are not motivated by 'advancement'. They are probably frustrated by their old jobs.

But when it comes to job creation, members of this group are unlikely to be unemployed when they decide to go it alone, or even when they first begin their new enterprise. They are the least likely to create many jobs, as their enterprise is very often to satisfy themselves. Even so, many Government policies seem to be aimed at this group.

High risk start-ups

It is a fact of life that the majority of the unemployed come from the lower income groups. So any who decide to work for themselves are most likely to start up in trades which do not need much capital investment, in their own home localities, and generally amid fierce competition from similar businesses. They are more likely to go under through lack of working capital, but even if they survive they are unlikely to grow.

Least help for lowest investment

Most such businesses are started by people not seeking a large income or with dreams of getting rich quick but seeking to earn a livelihood as good as their benefits, or better if possible. *But such people have traditionally had no help in their struggle to build up something from nothing.* In fact, the way benefit systems penalise them if they try, they have a powerful incentive either to work illegally or do nothing, since even small earnings can result in loss of benefits.

Enterprise allowances

However, there is one light at the end of the tunnel: the **enterprise allowance scheme** enables people who can invest at least £1,000 in a new business enterprise to have a Government allowance of £46 per week for the first year. There are very few strings attached, and it is a reasonable way to try to mobilise local potential.

Raising capital

The reality is that it is much easier to get hold of say £250,000 than it is to get a loan of £10,000–£50,000. This may seem ridiculous, but there is a whole trail of failed business people who will tell you that they cannot understand why their bank let a superb business opportunity go by the board for the sake of a miserable £10,000. A quick look at the various schemes which exist for providing capital for business makes it clear how this gap happens at the lower end of the market.

The small loan or overdraft

These are made by banks. They always require some sort of personal guarantee, such as your house, or other investment, and the rates of interest in the past few years have been crippling. Banks usually require a cash-flow forecast too (see the next chapter). This is probably the most common form of small loans, and the easiest to obtain at this level. But it is also a high risk, since you can be left with no home.

Loan guarantee scheme

This was supposedly set up to back high-risk enterprises which conventional sources such as banks would not back. The main banks never liked the scheme, and my own experience has been that it would be easier to ask the bank for the numbers on their combination locks than to get them to use the scheme! The banks have to put it forward and carry 30 per cent of the liability, so this way is blocked for most applicants. As if that is not enough discouragement, there is a Government premium of 2.5 per cent on top of the usual interest rates, (but watch for budget changes).

It is generally agreed that the Consumer Credit Act of 1985 imposed administrative problems which make loans of less than £15,000 virtually impracticable. Small wonder this scheme is moribund.

Business expansion scheme

This is more like it, we may think, if we are already in business and hope to expand. People who want to invest in other people's small businesses can gain tax advantages by putting up to £40,000 in unquoted companies. But the areas needing it most are not getting it. In 1983/4 the south-east alone attracted 53 per cent of individual investment, whereas the Midlands attracted only 13 per cent with very little if any of it going into small, high-risk investments. It has the *potential* for creating jobs quite cheaply compared with other methods (about £10,000 for each job created to date).

Effects of personal life on business

Mind you, if your personal finances are in a mess, or you're involved in a personal crisis such as separation or divorce, you're also a high risk and unlikely to come through a rough period of business activity. The commitment of your spouse to your enterprise, and the quality of your relationship (whether or not he or she is actively helping the business or just giving moral support) is crucial to success or failure, all other factors being equal.

The power of positive failures

No experience needs to be wasted. Many, if not the majority, of successful businessmen, have arrived where they are through learning from their experiences in at least one previous failure in a business. Experience can almost always be turned to good advantage for learning, whether it involves moonlighting or a more conventional route. Almost all research and surveys show that in the months during ie start-up of a new business or other enterprises for a community, those who are doing it learn an enormous amount which is useful to them for years to come.

'I will and I can.' Have you got what it takes?*

Motivation

To be successful, an entrepreneur must be really keen to achieve his or her ambition.

People with a high level of motivation, but with few skills, or no access to them, will be blocked in their ability to grow unless they can bring in help or get training. Those with skills and competence, but who are low on motivation, will probably survive but not expand. The fact is that small business is not an activity for the faint hearted, or someone looking for a substitute '9 to 5' job.

There is really no golden rule or measure to identify those who are likely to succeed. Those who have succeeded have a wide variety of backgrounds and personalities.

Politicians and civil servants often seem to assume that all that holds back hordes of would-be entrepreneurs are marginal tax adjustments or legal controls. In fact it is not money which is the main incentive for businessmen, it is only a means to an end and a measure of achievement.

Entrepreneurs are born – and made

A relative of mine, when a boy aged 8 or 9 years in 1943, came into the house one day and asked his father for a 'pair of scissors and some bits of string'. His father tried to find out why he wanted them, but the boy gave only vague replies about having 'an idea'. That evening he came home with ten shillings—a comparative fortune in 1943. He had gone around the gardens of bombed houses in his district in north London, cut the flowers, tied them into bunches and sold them door-to-door.

*I am indebted to Dr John Gill, Reader in Management Studies at Sheffield City Polytechnic, with Roger Green for some of the following.

That sort of story leads many people to believe that people are either born with entrepreneurial flair or they aren't, and that no amount of business studies or management training will make you into an entrepreneur if you aren't born with that flair.

If you are looking for a 9 to 5 job with a safe income, then trying to set up on your own is unlikely to produce it. If you are unsure, there are one or two things you could do to find out:

- *Think about what gets you going.* Do you enjoy competitive sports or games? Do you like board games or card games with an element of risk and competition, e.g. Monopoly? Poker? Remember one of the basic principles of business is that the greater the risk people take with their money, the bigger the return they expect to get. That's why you can't expect to get as much return from National Savings or a Building Society investment as you would from the Stock Market—there's very little risk in National Savings, other than interest rates being lower than the rate of inflation.

- *Go and talk to people already in business*—see if you like the kind of life they lead, and the things they have to do to keep it going. Find out how they started and what they found out in the early stages. It's no use asking many of them too much about their actual trading, most of them dislike sharing such information as they fear competition. You may not get much change from approaching strangers, but you could get a reasonable picture from relatives in business, or friends. This might infect you with some of the excitement and possibilities—or it might put you off completely.

In the end, what it boils down to is that if you've got the interest and drive you might succeed. If you haven't, no amount of training in business theory will make much difference.

Space agency!

No, not trying to compete with NASA, but a scheme whereby one organisation owns or leases a large building and others rent from it only as much space as they need to run their operation. This may vary from a voluntary organisation which needs only a desk for a part-time organiser, to a small firm which occasionally needs to hire a conference room.

This facility is still not very widespread, but it is an enormous help to small organisations, and particularly for new firms in their 'start-up stages'. Instead of having to take out a long lease—often for premises which are not entirely suitable or which have more space than is needed—only the holding organisation holds the lease. Individuals or groups rent what they need on a monthly basis.

Services are provided centrally, so that tenants pay only for what they use, whether typing, telephone answering, reception, refreshments, duplicating, telex, translation, photocopying, videos or conference rooms. Tenants can have their own telephone lines, but a facility can be built in whereby a line can be switched through to the control reception so that it is never left unanswered.

In an 'open plan' arrangement (such as in a converted warehouse), some tenants can literally be using nothing more than a desk space, perhaps with a free-standing panel behind them to hang a calendar or wall chart on. In buildings without open plan facilities, two or three different firms or voluntary bodies can be sharing one room.

'The more we are together'

A real feature of this space lease is the amount of help users give each other! There is a really clubby atmosphere in some such places, and the loneliness of the long distance entrepreneur is avoided. Tenants seek advice from each other, hire from each other, buy from each other, book seats or travel tickets and generally give each other support and encouragement.

When something like 40 per cent of all new businesses fail in their first year, to be able to reduce the liability of the person taking the risk to just a month's rent, instead of a 5-year lease must be helpful, to say nothing of the advantages gained by not having capital tied up in office equipment. A new user can move in within 24 hours! Such a person is not caught in the 'telephone trap'—'do I hire a part-time assistant I don't really need in case the phone rings while I'm out, or do I stay in myself (in which case I don't go out to get business), or do I leave the office empty and risk losing business because nobody answers?'

The central reception and answering facilities give callers and clients an important impression of the status and durability of the people they are dealing with. The renters themselves get support and encouragement in what is often a very lonely, risky and sleep-losing situation.

The principle is also very useful for voluntary organisations, and groups like pre-school playgroup associations. Help the Aged, CRUSE, Tenants' Federations, Marriage Guidance and Victim Support Groups often use such premises. Other interested bodies can include companies thinking of opening a regional office, but who don't want to commit themselves to a long lease until they know it is going to be an economically sound decision.

An area of some 500 square metres is needed if the operation is to stand on its own feet financially, but you would get away with less if the operation is a marginal one in premises where the costs are already covered by other activities. Rents charged start from about £30 per week just for a desk space. That usually includes rates, water, cleaning, electricity, reception, message taking, and mail franking and posting. Any other services are paid for if and when used.

Franchises

Franchises, sometimes referred to as 'off-the-peg' businesses, have grown tremendously in the past few years. Numbers have risen from approx 2,500 in 1950 to about 8,000 in 1984. One reason for this is that the risk of failure is lower than for a traditional new business start-up. But beware, because something is successful in London or Chicago, does not mean that York or Manchester will take to it in the same way! There are no really accurate figures available for the failure rate of franchise businesses.

Basically, what happens in franchising is that when a company has established a successful business operation and identity, it allows other people to operate the same operation under the same name, under licence. Usually the conditions state that the original operator (known as the *franchisor*) has the right to lay down exactly the format which the licensed operator (the *franchisee*) will use. This will include advertising material, shop fronts and displays (if applicable), goods sold, letterheads and stationery used, to exact specification, and accounts kept.

In return for what you hope will be a successful and tested business format, you have to pay the franchisor an initial payment. In addition you either have to buy your stock only from the franchisor, or, if you are in a service business which does not sell goods, but may buy all or part of its stock for example in the form of fresh fruit and vegetables daily, you have to pay the franchisor a 'royalty' based on *turnover*, not on profit.

Some of the best known franchise operations are Prontaprint and other high street print shops, Wimpy Bars, Little Chefs, Proud Potato and Kentucky Fried Chicken, Home Tune and British School of Motoring.

The British Franchise Association estimates that 90 per cent of franchising operations in this country bought from reputable companies succeed, but this does not indicate how many companies there are which are not members of the BFA. The purchase of a franchise can cost you as little as £2,000, and up to and over £200,000.

●

On the positive side, a franchise can be a good investment for a legacy or redundancy money (though some franchisors doubt if redundant executives have the necessary drive for a franchise), and a way of being your own boss without the usual risks attached to self-employment. Some franchises do have considerable scope and freedom for creativity and imagination within the limitations set down by the franchisor.

On the other hand, an individualist who resents too much restriction or limitation on how he trades would be well advised to steer clear of a franchise. In addition, if you are buying a label to market something you already know how to do quite well, you could well find yourself becoming highly resentful at paying out a percentage of your turnover each month to a franchisor. Having been both a franchisee and managed a franchise from scratch myself, I have seen the pros and cons.

If you want to try a franchise and are not sure how to go about it, there are one or two steps you can take to help. From your newsagent you can order the magazine *Franchise World*, published monthly. This contains a list of many of the major franchises (but not all). It also has articles and reports on new trends or activities. There is also the British Franchise Association which holds an annual National Franchise Exhibition (see the list of references at the end of Chapter 7). This is a worthwhile exhibition to visit as it is the only opportunity to see a wide range of franchises under one roof. It is usually held in October or November.

Co-operatives

In the past 10 years the number of people starting up co-operatives has grown considerably, although they are not as easy to run as we might think. We tend to find it difficult to build on one another's ideas.

We encourage young children to collaborate to learn in modern infant schools, with integrated day and family grouping. But at secondary level teenagers are actively taught *not* to collaborate to learn. So when it comes to working as a team in an office, in sales, on a shop floor, or in a voluntary committee, they have to learn new skills, and a vast army of trainers has sprung up to cash in on this need!

Unfortunately there is also resistance to co-ops from some trade unions who see them as a threat to their numbers. They find it difficult to see how co-operatives fit in with no clear 'boss' and hierarchy. And people in co-operatives are less likely to need the services of a trade union in its bargaining role. It also has to be said that some co-ops undercut union rates in order to gain business.

Officials

Co-operatives now exist for a range of activities, from housing to whole food. There is also a type of co-operative for savings and loans which I shall describe later. The Co-operative Development Agency is a government-funded agency which exists to advise on starting a new co-operative activity. It has officers in all major cities around the country, but don't assume that there is a tap waiting to be opened to let loose a flood of funds! However, advice is free and CDA officers can often help locate funds and give advice on the rules, criteria and legal obligations for setting up a co-op.

Skills

It is not enough to assume that because you have a group who are keen to start, know what area they want to work in, and seem to have similar values, that you will work harmoniously and successfully. Different people join such groups for different reasons (often unstated). Some jobs in a group are never popular: others appeal to everybody. Village communes have broken up because of an imbalance of males to females, or because only one or two people would dig the gardens. At a home craft co-operative there was conflict between those whose commitment was at the 'hobby' level and others who wanted to earn an income. Some find it difficult to get anybody who wants to keep the books and accounts; some have a heavy social interest, while others are mainly interested in the political side, and so on. Setting common objectives, working out who will do what, where the gaps or overlaps are, and talking them out, setting up internal decision-making and communication systems that work, and resolving inter-personal problems, take skills which sometimes have to be brought in.

Some examples

We shall now look at some examples of how others have fared with co-operatives, which may give you some ideas.

A co-operative from home

Margaret Elliott, a Sunderland resident, became enthused with the co-operative ideal when her husband was invited to join one. They quickly found it was a challenge to their way of life, not just another job. Challenged by the leading light in her husband's co-operative to do something for women, she and others first of all set up a shop with an upstairs crèche to enable members to help one another to work. The shop ran for three years, and although it sold ordinary groceries the women would break down packages into small portions for pensioners. Sheer economics decided them to close down in 1980.

Margaret took a course on co-operatives at Sunderland Polytechnic for a year, then looked to set up another one. After much discussion and searching, she and her friends found that there is a social services 'special needs' provision for an allowance for domestic help, particularly for the elderly. This provision is not tied in with the home help services provided by the local authority.

Margaret was fortunate enough to find the local DHSS officials themselves co-operative, and she and her colleagues set up a facility whereby a member of her co-operative (known as Little Women) visits the prospective client and assesses whether the person would be eligible for the special needs allowance. If so, the member fills in a short form, signed by the client, requesting help, and another which gives the co-op's representative's own assessment. When the DHSS receive these they visit the elderly person and assess how many hours' work are needed each week. The going rate (currently, £2.40 per hour) is paid to the client, who in turn pays this to the cleaner from Little Women. The co-operative takes a small administrative fee; the rest is kept by the one member who does the cleaning.

It is essential to realise two things about this scheme:

- the client, the elderly person, needs help, but for a variety of reasons does not qualify for home help from the local authority;

- most of the clients do not realise that this facility exists. If they did, they would find a cleaner by going to the Job Centre, or asking neighbours, as people do elsewhere.

In other words, they did not set out to privatise existing home help workers, and they have been careful not to undercut the rates paid by that service. All the women are members of NUPE, and the local shop steward was involved from the start by an agreement between NUPE, Little Women and the Sunderland Council. Some councillors were initially worried that this was 'back door privatisation' and had to be convinced that it was not, even though it could be shown that such cleaning services have never been other than private. A strong selling point was that Little Women are not undercutting home helps, either in the rates charged for cleaning or in the rates paid to their members.

Perhaps the strongest point in this activity is that the co-operative has identified funds which were not being made available, through lack of knowledge. They are providing help to people who could not otherwise receive it, and are bringing in money from a source not previously identified.

However, in its first two years, the co-operative needed a grant from the Local Authority to cover the costs of administration. Nobody is going to get rich, but jobs have been created. Sunderland's own home help service is stretched to the limit, so nobody is working at the expense of another person's job.

Cleaning businesses
Other people have found that cleaning can be profitable, working either alone, with employees, or with partners.

Some have specialised from the start, and this seems to be one key to a successful start-up. For example, instead of doing general hourly cleaning for the same people each week, some specialise in *whole house cleaning* for people who, say, have just finished redecorating, who have just moved, or who just want a good and thorough 'spring clean'. You can charge £15 for cleaning up after removers, or as much as £45 for a spring clean, depending on the size of the house and just how dirty it is. Cleaning a *cooker or refrigerator,* for example, can be a messy business and worth £4–5 hourly. It's worth getting hold of good materials to make the job easier.

Carpet and curtain cleaning can also be very profitable. It's surprising how few people can be bothered to do it themselves, or rather, how many would rather bring somebody else in. It takes about £1,000 to buy a really good carpet cleaner, and you need money for shampoos and local advertising, but at £15–20 per time for a complete semi-detached, plus extra for cleaning upholstery (using the same machine with different attachments), there is an income to be made, though again not a fortune.

A regular contract with a store, or for a suite of offices is obviously useful as these provide a regular income, and those paying can deduct the expense from tax, which the private householder cannot.

You need transport for your equipment for this work, but in a town it may be more economic to hire a taxi than run a car or van especially, unless you can do your own servicing. If you already have a car, Inland Revenue are quite agreeable to your claiming a generous proportion of the running costs as a legitimate business expense. If you are doing contract cleaning for business premises, you may well be able to negotiate a deal which includes transport costs.

Bed and breakfast

If you own your own house in an area where housing is expensive, you could think either of providing *bed and breakfast* for short-stay guests in that area, or buying a house with spare bedrooms elsewhere in an area more attractive to tourists.

You would need to fit wash basins in the bedrooms, and probably a second bathroom. After that you register with the English Tourist Board and advise your local Tourist Information Centre of your existence. Some advertising is also useful in the early stages, but if you provide a good service your best adverts will be personal recommendations and repeat visits. £18 per night for a double room with breakfast is quite common—more in some places, less in others.

Breeding at home—Open to misinterpretation, but read on!

A company known as Hyline Rabbits in Marston, Northwich (Cheshire) will buy rabbits which are 8–10 weeks old and weigh 2 kg (4½ lbs).

All you need to do is to buy a breeding female for £10, or preferably several, and one buck. Each female can produce 45 baby rabbits each year. They cost very little to feed and look after. Rabbits like lawn clippings, cauliflower or cabbage trimmings, bits from pot plants and ordinary kitchen scraps, almost anything in fact that humans don't eat, which is what makes them so cheap to bring up.

Each breeding doe generates an income of about £100 a year if it produces 45 babies, although there is also a new breed of big black rabbit which nearly doubles that output! Hyline collects them alive and they go to proper slaughter houses, so you are not involved in killing or skinning. Most of the meat is exported, as the British are not great rabbit eaters, and export prices are better.

Free range eggs are also much in demand, and can be profitable. However they do need land, some capital and expertise.

The waste industry

Experiences of making money from waste vary enormously. In Leeds and London there are schemes which make a profit out of waste and employ more people each year. They have been successful mainly because the local authorities concerned have adopted a positive attitude to the problem, and have helped small enthusiastic enterprises to get started.

The former GLC's *Recyclers' Guide to Greater London* takes the view that if it could achieve 20 per cent recycling of domestic and commercial waste, this would create 4,500 jobs. At present the figure is only around 4 per cent, and it is mostly only voluntary groups which make money out of recycling because all their labour is voluntary.

Some groups such as Friends of the Earth co-operate with the MSC's Community Programme on job-creation schemes. Their objective is to increase and improve the use of waste and recycling rather than to create permanent jobs. They have been particularly successful at this in Bristol where Resource-saver Ltd started up in 1981 after the local authority ceased collecting waste paper separately from other rubbish. By the end of 1985, Resource-saver employed nearly 40 people. They took on some of the Council's waste lorries (which proved an expensive liability), but a feature of their collections is two horse-drawn carts.

Resource-saver not only collect paper; their rounds pick up almost anything—rag, textiles, wool, sump oil. They also have a business which uses scrap wood to make small items sold locally, and they renovate old furniture which is sold to community groups and people on limited incomes. Finally they operate a Children's Scrapstore—a place where local companies dump anything they were going to throw out which may be of value to someone else, particularly people who run playgroups, schools or other activities for the young on a limited budget.

All these operations use people funded by the MSC's Community Programme, but Friends of the Earth's long-term aim is to work towards a more co-ordinated national policy. They believe that given the financial incentives found in countries such as Switzerland, Germany or New Zealand, re-processing plants could be funded which would create many more permanent jobs.

A recycling co-operative

One group which has been successful in creating permanent jobs is Blackwell Products, a co-op in Woolwich, south London. They have six staff who convert waste plastic barrels (used to import fruit and fruit juices) into compost units for gardens. The barrels are washed out, drilled in the appropriate places, then spray painted. Each one is then set in an aluminium frame designed to allow the barrel to rotate. It is called the Tumbler. Kitchen waste and grass clippings can be turned into good quality compost in 21 days.

The Tumbler was launched in March 1985 with a £50,000 loan from the Greater London Enterprise Board, and by the end of 1985 sold more than 1,000 tumblers per month, well above the predicted sales. Blackwell anticipates running into profit in its second year, but as compost making is seasonal Blackwell Products is trying out other products. One area of development is collecting and cleaning bottles from wine bars for resale to home brewers.

Look around

I am constantly amazed at how people manage to spot some corner of a market and fill it themselves. By far the majority of new small enterprises are services, very few are manufacturing. It is worth buying some of the 'quality' Sunday newspapers or mid-week papers which have business reviews, or see them in the public library where they are free. They often publish stories of individuals or small groups of people who have had an idea and brought it to market, sometimes even by accident. I remember being stimulated over the years by stories like the following:

- The band of strugglers who designed and made men's ties, with so little space to work that one of them operated a sewing machine seated on the w.c.

- The couple who made it sound as though they had a small factory by having a cassette recording of busy factory noises which was turned on whenever the telephone was picked up—in their own home.

- The people who actually hired factory space for a couple of days and used it instead of their makeshift premises to make a good impression on a chain store buyer, so as to obtain orders.

- The two ladies who started from home, making pizzas for their local small shops and within 6 months had a dozen people hard at work supplying supermarkets in their own and nearby towns.

- The journalist who cashed in on his travels around the country and supplemented them to complete information for a book about where you can get a decent and reasonable meal by leaving the motorway.

- The people I know, and whose services I have used, who make frozen food dishes to order by telephone and deliver them to the door. They are superb 'home cooking' and contain none of the preservatives or artificial colouring of supermarket equivalents.

- The couple who did a door to door survey in their area of a city to find out what the people felt they lacked by way of retail trade. The answer they came up with—a bookshop, which they opened and which is flourishing.

- The two ladies who hired a carpet shampooing kit one weekend to clean their own houses and found their friends wanted theirs done too and were willing to pay for it. This laid the foundation for them buying their own equipment and hiring themselves out.

- The redundant electrician with 3 small children who looks forward to the sight of dirty nappies. For 0.5p each he will loan you 40, collect them when soiled and lend you 40 clean ones. Those who use the service do not have to buy nappies and do not have the problem of getting them dry again in time to wear.

- The wife of a steel company executive who was asked to do some laundry for a buyer visiting from overseas. On enquiring she found that even quite large hotels, and none of the small ones in her town had any laundry service, and stepped in, first using her own machine, then the launderette, finally installing 2–3 machines and a drier in a spare room.

The important thing is not to go into something which others are already doing successfully nearby. Reading through other people's experiences in other towns may well give you an idea for something which is not happening in your part of the world. Whatever you do, make sure you are covered by insurance for yourself and third parties. If you are going to do it seriously, there are a few other things to think about too, as we shall see in the next chapter.

Further Reading

All of these books are written for beginners and small business entrepreneurs, not for library shelves or Business School essays.

Work for Yourself by Paddy Hall
Published by NEC and Shell U.K. Ltd. Small Business Unit

Full of lots of good ideas and useful contacts. Also has more comprehensive information on co-operatives and the different approaches needed when making things, selling them, or producing a service.

The Small Business Kit Several Authors Published by NEC

Guardian Guide to Running a Small Business edited by Clive Woodcock Published by Kogan Page

Daily Telegraph Guide to Self-Employment by Godfrey Golzen Published by Kogan Page

Franchise World   Quarterly Magazine   Order from: James House, 237 Nottingham Road, London SW17 7EA

The Collective Housing Handbook   by Sarah Eno and Dave Trevor   Laurieston Hall Publications

Co-ops: A Directory of Industrial and Service Co-operatives from Co-operative Development Agency, 20 Albert Embankment, London SE1 7TJ. 01-211 4633

Mail Order List

Books about Worker Co-operatives can be obtained from your nearest Co-operative Development Agency or from London ICOM, 7 Bradbury Street, London NI6. 01-249 2837

The Careers and Occupational Information Centre (COIC) of the Manpower Services Commission has publications on self-employment including:

Down to Business   by Gary Phillips

All Our Own Work Published by COIC in the Learning To Earn Series
Address: COIC Sales Dept., FREEPOST, Sheffield S1 4BR

Community Business Works. Report by Calouste Gulbenkian Foundation, 98 Portland Place, London W1N 4ET.

⬛8 Money, Money, Money

Introduction

This chapter is not exclusively for those planning business operations, nor for voluntary groups. Some will apply more to one or the other, but much is common ground for both.

I shall not provide a comprehensive guide to business book-keeping or money management. First, I shall point out the need to take advice and to keep at least simple records yourself. I shall try to demystify some phrases such as *the business plan* and *cash flow*, and even the dreaded VAT—and to show that there are positive aspects of these activities.

I shall highlight some of the reasons why many businesses fail, and where to go for help if you are in trouble with your books. Inevitably, problems arise whenever more than one person has to handle cash or goods, and I shall suggest simple but well tested ways in which losses from careless handling, or through deliberate attempts to defraud, can be kept to a minimum.

In the second section, I shall examine the sources of a variety of grants from the EEC and Government agencies for business, and from charities and trusts for a wide variety of purposes. I shall suggest ways of getting advice on how to apply for them, which can cost nothing.

Finally, I shall suggest a way in which a community or other interested group can be encouraged to avoid paying the heavy interest rates currently operating through banks or finance companies for loans or hire purchase, and in the process assist people who would not qualify for hire purchase through conventional channels, except at very high rates of interest.

Buddy can you spare a dime?

One common feature of my experiences with people in business for themselves is their reluctance to seek out and accept advice on the use of their money, record how it is being used, or how it could be used more effectively.

There are a number of reasons why people do not seek advice, including such things as:

- They may be worried that if they seek professional or more experienced advice their project will be condemned before it starts, and they fear this type of rejection.

- They may not like someone else to see exactly how flimsy their financial status is (which usually means they will not even admit it to themselves either).

- They may not know who to trust to give them the advice they need, especially at the start-up stage. They may well be justified in their reservations. Not all high street bank managers or qualified accountants have any experience in, or even of accounting for, a small business.

- Some businessmen do not keep very good records, if any. They stuff copy invoices and receipts into tins or desk drawers, and only put records together when someone like the VAT Office or Inland Revenue threatens them with court action, or demands more than they believe they should pay. They are too embarrassed to approach a good book keeper or accountant directly and try to put something together themselves, to cover up the mess.

The business plan

Sounds formidable! It conjures up visions of complicated sets of figures and glossy brochures put out by large companies, and elegantly printed materials on boardroom tables in TV epics, usually accompanied by glossy wall charts and architects' models!

Forget it—most plans for small businesses start with someone putting their thoughts down, starting on a piece of scrap paper or the back of an envelope. Later these thoughts are developed and polished up for a bank manager, but ordinary typing, nicely spaced, is quite adequate.

But don't make the mistake of thinking that such plans are an exercise only for bank managers. Many an entrepreneur with what seemed a good idea has had to come to the reluctant conclusion that it was not practical when he or she has sat down and asked . . .

What and Why and How
And Where and When and Who?

The purpose is not to kill off the idea, but

- to test it out theoretically and to your own satisfaction before spending money on it;

- to set it out in a way that will explain the proposal and its implications to other people—that means it must be logical in its layout, and well organised;

- to show the bank that you have thought the proposal through carefully and responsibly—even if the proposal itself is unusual;

- to provide a base from which you can project, especially if it is to be used to raise money, and anticipate what will happen and meet changes—in other words, to help control and maintain progress.

Different people will lay out the information in different ways, but all contain the same basics. The following sequence has always seemed to me to be logical and the main principles are well tried, tested and accepted.

Start with a summary

If you watch busy people who pick up a report, they very often turn to the end to see if there is a summary—so put it in first on the front page. Make sure it is a summary, and not just the report given differently and nearly as long!

What it must show is:

- what you are trying to do—your objectives;

- what it is you are hoping to sell, make or do, how it will be done, and what makes it special or distinguishable from others;

- what the 'market potential' is, who you'll be competing with, and where: e.g. if your service is to householders, a visit to the

Town Hall or reference library can tell you how many households are in the area, while Yellow Pages or Chamber of Commerce will be a guide as to how many other firms or individuals are doing the same thing or similar;

- who is going to manage and do the work, and whether their skills or experience are relevant;

- the finance needed, how it will be spent, what income and returns can be expected, and when.

What you have above is the basis for the full report. You can get a full exposition of a complete plan from some of the books I mentioned in the previous chapter, or you can get free advice by obtaining a booklet or pamphlet on the subject from a bank, or one of the leading firms of accountants. If you are planning to produce something, a small colour photograph of the product will be helpful.

In practice you will find you cannot write the summary until you have written the full proposal. But this will then be a key tool for managing if you have done it properly—particularly from the financial section which will tell you such things as:

- whether your costs are running above or below estimates;

- whether your products are being turned out above or below expectation;

- what levels of sales will be required to break even (cover costs including your salary), and to make a profit.

The great thing is not to kid yourself. Don't try to trim your figures to fit your view of what you *want* to happen!

Help—we're sinking!

It is generally agreed that there are two main reasons which cause small businesses to collapse. The same reasons very often lead voluntary organisations into difficulties, and have caused several to close down. In technical terms, these problems are known as:

Cash flow

At the basic level of everyday operations, the usual symptom of this problem is either that you cannot meet a bill (such as gas or supplies), or you cannot buy the materials you need to keep producing, because someone who owes you money has not paid you, or, worse still, you think you have enough cash in the bank to issue a cheque for materials, only to have your cheque bounce and an irate supplier on your neck or putting you into bankruptcy.

Either way, it is because the cash flowing out has been faster than that flowing in. The size of the debt is not always that important. Many an entrepreneur has been in despair when he or she has managed to have one supplier hold off who is owed quite a large amount—say £1,000—only to find he is being sued by someone who is owed £75.

Lack of working capital

This is the sure sign of an inadequate business plan. It means that before you start earning an income from sales or service, you have run out of cash to pay the staff, buy materials, place advertisements, or even buy postage stamps.

Very often this is brought about because you have used working capital to buy small items of equipment—tools, office furniture, a typewriter. Such items should not be bought with working capital—it is more in your favour to use other people's money by getting a loan for them.

If you do get into problems, they will not just melt away. See the next section on stewardship for ideas on where to go for help.

Stewardship

You don't need me to tell you that money for projects is scarce and getting scarcer all the time. So those who give grants are constantly on the lookout to make sure they are not going to fund a group who don't have the management skills to look after money or draw up a budget and know both where the money will go and where it has gone; who don't suddenly wind up their activities because nobody took account of the need to meet the bill for rent, rates or gas.

There is quite a lot of help available if you look around. A number of local authorities, adult education centres, and Councils for Voluntary Services now lay on training programmes, and in other places there are specialist agencies to assist, for example, Nottingham Action Resource Centre has a Community Accountancy Support Service: a small team provides free auditing and a free 'rescue service' in book-keeping. They also run training sessions for entrepreneurs and voluntary groups. Leicester CVS has a team of book-keepers on 'rescue work' for those who have got into a muddle.

Hackney Community Accountancy Project has produced a splendid booklet called *How to manage your money—if you have any*. A computer programme is also being designed based on this book. Contact

HACKNEY CAP,
34 Dalston Lane,
London E8 3AZ (£1.25 + 25p post)

or

Accounting and Financial Management for Charities
Directory of Social Change,
9 Mansfield Place,
London NW3 1HS (£5.95)

It is much more difficult to check and evaluate the value of a project to a community, than to check its finances. Oddly, the voluntary sector has been slower to take on what is known as a 'social audit' than some of our major commerical companies, who have come to realise that there is more to contribute to society than just making money for shareholders. But you can't begin a social audit if you don't look after your cash—you won't last long enough!

VAT – not a four-letter word!

One of the first myths that has grown up among people who have never dealt with Value Added Tax is that it is a terrible administrative burden to a small business or charitable trust carrying out trading through sales. People think it is complicated to record, and therefore increases overhead costs.

So there is continued pressure for thresholds to be raised (i.e. the trading figure set by Customs and Excise from the Treasury at which it becomes compulsory to register for VAT. At present this stands at a turnover of £20,500 per annum). Many small business people would not dream of registering until they reach this threshold, and some believe they would not be allowed to.

While it may suit some politicians to blow trumpets about this alleged burden (one which most of them have not experienced, except as tax payers!), in reality, as with many myths, the opposite is true. There are very definite advantages—financial and controlling—both to you and your customers in registering as early as possible. Also, as long as you keep receipts and payment vouchers in good order, it is certainly the easiest of taxes to administer. VAT records can provide a basis for putting together your monthly accounts later. My experience is that Customs and Excise staff are extremely helpful, and believe me, I need help!

Start-up advantages

One of the advantages of registering for VAT when you first open up, or from the day you buy your first ballpoint pen and paper, is that you can claim back from VAT all the tax you have paid out on start-up capital equipment such as office furniture and equipment, computers, tools, kitchen equipment or any other fittings and fixtures (but not cars or vehicles for some reason).

VAT accounts are done quarterly. So if trading is slow at first, or your first few weeks are spent more in kitting up and production than selling or providing services, your refund from VAT may be nearly as much, or more than your payments. I know of one business that went badly and folded within 3 months. The VAT refund cheque was nearly £1,000 more than the businessman had collected from customers, so the unhappy man could pay off some debts.

It seems to me a false economy to delay registering for VAT until after the start-up period, during which time your expenditure on refundable items is heaviest. But beware! The exception is a business which supplies on credit. You have to pay VAT on the invoice, not the receipt, so you may pay VAT on a bad debt, as does happen.

Keeping the VAT record

A great advantage of this tax, as I said earlier, is that everything you buy or sell has to be recorded regardless of whether or not it carries VAT. So if your monthly or annual accounts are done by an accountant or book-keeper, all *you* have to do is record each item daily on two sheets of paper (a proper book for recording can be bought at most office suppliers):

1. *input* record of *purchases* of materials, expenses or overheads;

2. *output* record of *sales*, work done, or services to customers.

The *input* record looks like this:

1st quarter		A	B	C	
	Serial	Inv.	VAT input	Item at standard	
Date	Supplier	No.	Total	tax	rate	Note
1.4	Computer Supplies Ltd	1	106.80	13.93	92.87 (hire purchase)
1.4	Fast Print Ltd	2	4.10		4.10 no VAT
1.4	Elec. Board	3	30.45		30.45 no VAT
2.4	Jackson Directories	4	33.50	4.37	29.13 (advertising)
30.6	O.K. Stationery	181	2.95	.38	2.57
	Total 1st Quarter		9,280.15	1,045.11	8,235.04
			A	B	C

Note Columns **A** less **B** = **C**. *Column B is the amount you can claim.*
(There is also a fourth column, but we need not expound on this here.)

This figure will be the highest for several quarters, since in the first period of trading you buy your equipment.

The principle is the same for the *output* record, except that you will be listing people or firms you have sold to, and the total at the end is of how much you owe the VAT man. So how does this benefit your customers? The possibilities are two-fold:

1. the customers who are registered for VAT themselves can claim this on their returns;
2. your overheads are reduced when you are able to claim back VAT on raw materials.

Of course, if you are not supplying traders with whatever you produce, the materials you use are free of VAT, and you have had little or no capital outlay, then there is no advantage in registering yourself.

105

Expansion

VAT is a very useful control if you are thinking of leaving somebody else to run your business for whatever reason, or are spreading it, or opening another branch, or starting a franchise—any situation, in fact, where you have to depend on someone else to run it.

While such a person may be tempted to rip *you* off in some way, in so doing he will also have to fiddle Customs and Excise, and the penalties for that are much more severe, including imprisonment.

On the fiddle

Regretfully, every so often a voluntary group or community organisation runs into a financial crisis, or finds itself unexpectedly short—not because it hasn't been successful at raising money or handling it, but because one or more members have been dipping their fingers in the till. This is more common than is often realised, and it is certainly more common than any one person taking off with the entire balance.

The reasons for this are fairly simple:

- by the very nature of what they are doing, the people running such groups are usually naive and inexperienced in keeping books of accounts and checking cash;
- book-keeping, money minding and checking are, rightly, not seen as the main purpose of the organisation.

Consequently the disciplines taken for granted in a commercial organisation (such as always checking cash on handover or takeover, or checking bank statements against receipts or membership records) are either not understood or are considered an embarrassing aspersion against other people's honesty.

It would not be practical to cover every eventuality or possible way in which a group can lose money or stocks, whether unintentionally, from carelessness, or through intentional fraud. Someone intent on fraud or theft can usually find a way. But it would be a pity to lose out and find yourselves unable to account for money simply because some simple basic procedures have been neglected. The following are guidelines.

Officials

- If possible, do not appoint a treasurer who does not have at least some experience of keeping a simple cash account. If you have nobody with such experience, don't just let it drift. Try to find somebody who does know something about it to show the treasurer what to do—somebody the treasurer can go back to and check with at intervals.

- Never appoint an honorary auditor who has no book-keeping experience, even if you have to go outside your organisation. In fact it's better to go outside if you can find someone to take it on. There will be no option at all about this point if you are receiving funds from outside sources, whether Government agencies or charitable trusts.

- The more people who handle cash or stocks (e.g. food, potato crisps, drinks), the more likely it is that something will go missing. In a situation where several people have to handle stocks or cash at once (e.g. serving in a community café), have only sufficient stocks and cash at the counters for the current trading session. One person only should be responsible at any time for collecting excess cash, and for issuing new stocks from stores.

A typical situation arose in a small society which for several years had held annual elections for officers, including the hon. treasurer, and every year had given the books to the hon auditor, a TV engineer, to check before the annual general meeting. One year the TV engineer resigned, and a bank clerk volunteered to take on the job, which was considered a formality.

Came the annual audit check, the treasurer handed the bank statements, receipt book and cash book to the auditor. The auditor checked these and found them correct as expected. He then asked for the membership register. After some initial resistance ('What do you want that for? It's never been wanted before'), and embarrassing insistence, the new auditor discovered that there were more members on the register than subscriptions paid into the bank. The next thing was the check on previous years' accounts, and the quiet resignation of the hon. treasurer!

Handling cash

- Always insist on counting out cash when handing it over to somebody else, and insist that other people do the same when handing cash over to you. Any amount handed over should always be noted down and initialled by the receiver.

- If you use a cash register or lock-up drawer for cash, always empty it at night and leave the drawer open to show that it is empty. If the amount of cash in hand overnight is more than a few pounds, have a night safe built in. It can be quite simple, a strong steel box cemented into the wall or under the floor, with a picture or rug over the top to deter the casual thief looking for easy pickings.

- Whoever locks the cash away should always include a note of how much is in the safe, and keep a separate note outside the safe. The float too should be locked up at the same time.

- Simple controls are the most effective. Keep a record of small daily transactions such as pints of milk, tea, or parking meters in a daily notebook, and enter the total weekly into the cash account. Either you initial the entry yourself, or the person who makes the purchase does. Larger purchases such as stationery or paint are entered into the cash account direct. The person who takes the cash to collect the milk or matches however should not be the same person that keeps the daily notebook.

- Don't overkill the petty cash records or nobody will want the job! Most auditors are quite satisfied with a signature on a notebook for a couple of pints of milk or a packet of sugar, and will not demand individual receipts and cash sale vouchers.

  The worst exception is any Government auditor. If you receive a grant which is auditable by the MSC, for example, instead of using a parking meter for 10p they will insist that you use a Local Authority or private car park where a receipt can be issued—which usually means a minimum of 40p. (Multiply that by the number of civil servants and others on official business who have to pay parking fees daily in our cities, and multiply that by 365. Add what it costs to check that they've done it properly and you probably have the annual running costs of a medium-sized NHS hospital!)

- It is better to check with your auditor that he agrees with your systems before getting too deep into them, than trying to adjust them at the end of the year when he throws up his hands in horror!

- Wherever possible, the person who makes payments, i.e. pays out cheques or issues cash, should not be the same person who keeps the records which show how much is to be paid, to a supplier, or in wages.

- Anyone in charge of paying money must keep a receipt or voucher for every payment. The vouchers should be numbered consecutively and kept.

Goods

- Keep items for sale or any other assets safely locked away. Release only what is necessary for sale or use during a limited period ahead—e.g. in a community shop, up to 2 days stock for sale.

- Only one person should have the key to a store and issue and receive goods.

- All goods received and all goods issued should be counted and agreed by both parties. Delivery drivers can be very sharp at times, don't take their word for anything. After all they won't accept yours and mistakes are *never* in your favour (at least not to any real value).

- Never hold more stocks than you need. If deliveries are made each week don't hold more than 10 days stock.

- Every item in stock should have what is known as a *bin card*. For example:

Item: Fizz Bars					Unit: Bars				
Date	in	out	bal.	sign.	Date	in	out	bal.	sign.
1/2	24	—	24	J.B.					
2/2	—	8	16	G.J.					
5/2	—	4	12	G.J.					

All items should be broken down to their smallest unit, e.g.:

24 Fizz bars (not 1 case);
or 36 bottles lemon pop (not 1 case).

By keeping careful records on cards in a short time you will

- have a picture of what sells and what does not, or what is used and what is not;
- be able to stop stocking items which don't move;
- see immediately if anybody is. taking something without paying.

Government grants (business)

There is a vast assortment of grants available from EEC, Government and local authority sources—the trick lies in getting your hands on them. There is quite a big element of discretion in many of the grant schemes, which can be a two-edged sword. On the one hand it means you could be helped even though you don't quite fulfil all the normal conditions; on the other hand, since civil servants are not paid to take risks, it also means that you might still be turned down even though you believe you have answered every question satisfactorily.

Although this seems like a 'heads we win, tails you lose' situation, it is worthwhile trying—the most unlikely groups do succeed. An important step is to contact the authority responsible for making the grant as early as possible in your planning, and certainly before you commit yourself to any lease of premises, loans from private sources or legally binding commitments.

How do you find out?

Many of the major banks, and firms of chartered accountants, now publish their own guides, for all types and sizes of business, to assistance available from Government for business and commerce.

For groups such as community groups, or those with other socially useful purposes, the situation is not so easy and it often means applying to the local authority for urban aid, or to charities and trusts, national or local.

For small business and co-operative start-ups or expansion it is worth your while contacting your bank or firm of accountants and asking to be put in touch with somebody on their staff who is a specialist in applying for government assistance. Most banks and accountants now have such specialists, having realised how much value these can give their clients, and that what keeps their clients afloat will be good for them too.

There is of course the newest of the goldmines, the Manpower Services Commission. By joining a community programme as a patron under an existing management sponsor, you may well obtain funding to pay some part-time workers at the current rate. But there are a number of snags:

- you have to make the *job description* fit the MSC criteria: this is not always easy since different areas and different MSC officers within an area often have different views as to how these should be interpreted, and have varying degrees of flexibility;

- once you are dependent on MSC funds it is difficult to become independent again—a number of worthy schemes have collapsed when the MSC have withdrawn recognition;

- bringing in paid part-timers to do the work volunteers once did has a powerful demotivating effect on any future voluntary activity. I have heard clergy complain that their congregation will no longer tackle simple church mainten- ance tasks as they expect community programme labour to do them.

What sort of grants or incentives for small business or business expansion?

Broadly speaking there are two types:

- **Regional incentives.** These follow the assumption that selected areas will be lifted out of their unemployment problems by encouraging firms to expand or set up within them. So designated areas qualify for Regional Development Grants, Regional Selective Assistance and the European Regional Development Fund. The latter has 'Non-quota' funds aimed at areas hit by the decline in the steel industry, and for environmental projects or small firm improvement. There are also designated Enterprise Zones, and other grants are made through assistance to local authorities and develop- mental agencies, such as the Council for Small Industries in Rural Areas (COSIRA), or the Welsh Development Agency.

- **Other incentive schemes.** These are designed to provide a range of assistance, both in grants and by consultancy, regardless of where your enterprise is located. There is a variety of funds for new innovation development—e.g. computer aided design and manufacture, software, industrial robots and the application of micro-electronics. There is support for investment in tourism and textiles. There are advisory services for design, energy efficiency and manufacturing, as well as for small firms. There is assistance for a variety of training schemes, whether for computers or the community programme.

Applying for help

The specialist officers I mentioned at banks and accountants' firms will not charge you for a preliminary discussion in which they can look at what you want help for and decide the appropriate funds to apply for.

If they help you put together an application, they may make a charge, but often they expect that this will be met by the grant being applied for.

However, it will be seen as normal business practice for you to ask them to clarify what is free and what you would have to pay for at an early stage in your discussions. If the grant application is not successful, your group may then be asked to pay for the work involved in preparing the application.

Another advantage of seeing an expert is that he can often refer you to more than one scheme, or advise you to proceed in such a way that you will qualify for other schemes. For example, you may qualify under the European Regional Development Fund, but applying for a particular site may also qualify you for a land reclamation grant.

Whichever way you want to go about it, virtually all assistance has to be applied for either through the Local Authority or the Department of Trade and Industry or Environment. The main exception to these are help from one of the development agencies, and training grants which are dealt with by the Manpower Services Commission.

The following notes are more applicable to community groups and organisations than to small business practice.

Charities and trusts

There are literally thousands of charities throughout the country. Some have fairly wide-ranging objectives; others are limited to very specific target groups, e.g. 'blind widows living within 1 mile of the parish church of St Gelfred's'. There are a number of directories of grant-making trusts. Some of these list the main grant-givers by the type of work they support, e.g. all those which support educational objectives are together.

A growing and helpful trend is the setting up of charity information services in the main cities and county towns throughout the country. Often funded by local authorities and urban aid grants they advise applicant groups which charities and trusts would be most appropriate to apply to. To do this effectively they also contact charities whose aims and conditions are unclear to clarify these.

Without this sort of help, doing it yourself can be a time consuming, expensive and heartbreaking business—with your carefully worded and typed letter, possibly with photographs, ending up in somebody's waste basket. If there is no such service in your area, your local reference library may hold some helpful information on local resources.

There are a number of guidelines which have proved useful when applying to charitable trusts:

- Keep it short, preferably within 1 sheet of A4, maximum 2 sides. The longer it is, the less likely it is to be read. Trustees are not paid officials and often receive a lot of applications. If they want more details they will come back to you.

- Have your application typed if possible, and include with it copies of your last set of audited accounts and annual report (unless you are just starting up).

- You should say if you are a registered charity yourself. Some trusts can give only to charities by the terms of their own constitutions. If you are not a charity, your best move may be to affiliate with an existing charity doing complementary but not competing work to what you are proposing.

- Make it clear what your group is or is not hoping to do, how much or what resources you need to do it, and why you are doing it. How you are organised, how long you have been formed, and who is involved will also be important information. Remember you will not get anything for a solo effort, and as I said in an earlier chapter, to have a couple of well known names with some credibility, as patrons on your list of trustees or sponsors, will certainly help.

- Include information as to who else has donated and how much. The temptation is to think that charities will not contribute if you already have money or goods from elsewhere, but in fact nothing succeeds like success. If you've had some assistance already, this helps your credibility and encourages others.

Very Important Information
- How do you raise funds for yourself? This is an area of increasing interest to charities, some of whom will look more favourably upon groups who show they have tried to help themselves before appealing to others.

- We're back to keeping it simple. Your 5,000 word report on the social deprivation of the tortoise in urban areas may be compelling reading, but don't send it—or anything else not strictly relevant to the application!

- Finally, you would be amazed at how many people fail to give even the simplest acknowledgement for cheques or donations they receive. Charities can have long memories, and if you haven't thanked them you will probably be wasting your time in going back to them later. They also need feedback on your success or failure, so that they can build up some data on their own effectiveness. Such feedback and acknowledgement can affect their attitudes to other applications similar to yours.

I wish to acknowledge the generous help of the South Yorkshire Charity Information Service in putting this section together.

There are a number of books which are very useful. Some are expensive, but they can almost always be viewed at your local reference library, or in the library of your local Council for Voluntary Services. They are:

- *Raising Money from Trusts*—Directory of Social Change.
    This gives far more detail on how to approach trusts and

how they operate. It also gives some comments and views by some of the bigger trusts.

- *Directory of Grant-Making Trusts*—Charities Aid Foundation.
  This is a major tome on grant-making trusts in Great Britain.

- *Charitable Status—A Practical Handbook*—Inter-Action Guides.
  A useful guide to the snags and benefits of registering as a charity and how to go about it.

- *Can you Credit it?*—Warren Feek, NYB
  It's always useful to have the views of the other side of the fence, and this is a useful insight into how some trusts view the organisations who apply to them, as well as describing how they deal with applicants.

The credit merry-go-round—and how to get off it

For the first time since records have been kept in Britain on consumer spending, average family savings have been overtaken by family debt, which is not healthy for family or country.

Len Nuttall, Chief Executive Officer
Association of British Credit Unions Ltd.

It is extraordinary that although borrowing money is probably as expensive as it has ever been legally, more is being borrowed for domestic purposes than ever before—through bank loans, credit cards issued by banks and large stores, finance houses and money lenders. This is resulting in an increasing number of family tragedies.

For example, the number of people 6–12 months in arrears with mortgage payments has trebled in the past 3 years. About 100,000 are more than 3 months behind in payments to building societies; over a million council tenants have rent arrears, and one and a half million gas and electricity consumers have problems paying their bills. Mrs Elizabeth Stanton, of the National Consumer Council, says that in most cases, 'it is not that people won't pay—they can't pay'.

For the unemployed, or others on limited incomes, the merry-go-round builds up like this:

```
      so                      so                    my
    I can                   I have               washing
    hardly    ────────▶       no      ────────▶  machine
    afford                  savings               breaks
      it                                           down
       ▲                                            │
       │                                            ▼
      so                      so                    so
 the machine              I have to pay         I have to
 costs much    ◀────────  a high rate of  ◀──── borrow to
 more than the              interest              replace
 price marked                                       it
```

SUNDAY MIRROR, January 24, 1988   PAGE 29

Sharks that gather around your home

I GET worried when I see moneylenders making ...

By City Editor
ROBERT HEAD

CONSOLIDATION LOANS
Pay off all outstanding credit cards, HP and existing loans etc and have one easy payment. Compare our examples with your present re-payments, you'll probably find you have cash to spare for those home improvements, holi...

LIVOOL ECHO — JAN 15th

Debt mountain is burying millions

MILLIONS of people in Britain are seriously in debt and a completely new system is needed to deal with them, it was claimed today. "It is time we stopped treating poor people, who can't pay their debts, almost as if they are criminals," said Mrs. Elizab... n, of the National Consumer Council. -

... debt," she told the first conference in Britain on debt and how to tackle it.

It was attended ...
lending i...

lawyers, fuel boards, money advice workers, government depart-ments and consumer ...nisations.

FAST PERSONAL LOANS £150–£150,000
24 HOUR SERVICE
ONE MONTH

FAST NO-NONSENSE LOANS
★ Free confidential advice
★ No obligation
Any purpose loans. Homeown...
mortgage payer...

Debt burdens
MORE than half of this country is in debt due to disturbing circum-stances such as unemployment, and all we keep hearing about is Heseltine, Hatton and helicopters. Many people whose circum-...'t make ends meet; ...h millstone mortgages ...ending debts. ...rerage person would be ...rested in being advised ...ich resolve their ... than ...

Arrears
...een 1986 and ...he number of ... to 12 months ...s with mort-...bled. About ...ouseholders ... than three ...nd with pay-...building

...a million ...nts were ...ents, one

How much more does credit cost?

By law nowadays a credit agreement has to tell you exactly how much you will be paying. Even so, for people who have no job there is not much option, as I discovered when I was a 'mature student' living in a Gateshead high-rise flat 3 years ago. I tried to hire a T.V. from a High Street retailer. When the store manager saw my occupation and my address he told me company policy would not allow me to hire the set—even though I offered him 6 month's advance rental on a credit card!

For people who actually *need* credit, the alternatives are limited, and are more expensive. Those lending charge much higher interest rates to insure against what they see as a higher risk. Take a look:

Suppose you borrow £500 to pay back over 24 months. Typical extra amounts in interest run currently as follows:

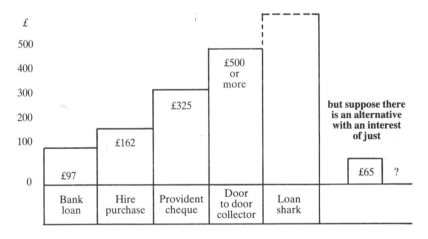

The good news is that there *is* just such an alternative—it is called a **Credit union.**

Because credit unions exist only to serve their members, loans cost only 1 per cent per month on any outstanding balance—this is just over 12 per cent per year. In other words you are charged only £6.50 pence for every £100 borrowed and repaid in equal instalments over 12 months. That is *five times less* than a Provident cheque.

So on the figures shown above, for a credit union loan of £500 for 2 years you would pay:

- *£32 less than a bank loan,*
- *£97 less than H.P.,*
- *£260 less than a Provident cheque,*
- *£435 less than some finance companies!*

So, among other things, credit unions increase their members' purchasing power, since members' money goes further.

Usury

At one time rates of interest were at a level mainly to cover the costs of lending. To lend money for the sake of making more money was considered immoral.

It is interesting to observe that strict Islamic banks and Orthodox Jews carry out this principle in their own dealings. By contrast, our Western, so-called Christian civilization has no compunction about wringing out the maximum possible interest from its own community. The poorer people are, the greater the rate of interest they have to pay.

What is a credit union?

A credit union can be thought of as a mutual self-help society: people who live, work, or play together pool and manage their savings to help themselves and to help each other, rather than paying financial institutions to do it. In other words, it is a money co-operative.

To call a society a credit union (rather than just a holiday savings club), it has to be registered with the Registry of Friendly Societies. To be accepted you have to show that:

- your members have an appropriate *'common bond';*
- you have the *usual objects* of a credit union;
- you have a *set of rules* which are acceptable to the Registrar;
- you have at least 21 members.

The common bond

The Credit Union movement has always held the view (borne out by experience) that the best protection possible against bad debts is the way that members can assess each others' credit worthiness when they are all part of some community or club, and have a mutual interest in not letting each other down.

The reality of this can be judged by the fact that their bad debts are less than a quarter those of banks (0.35 per cent to be precise, compared with the banks' 1.5 per cent). It seems that the very act of forming a credit union engenders stronger bonds of trust and loyalty than existed previously.

This common bond, which must be acceptable to the Registrar, means having a link of some kind, such as living or working in one particular street or area, belonging to a trade union, works organisation, or other organisation such as a church, social club or tenants' association.

The aims of a credit union are quite clear:
- to encourage thrift and to promote systematic savings by encouraging members to save part of their earnings each week;
- to eliminate usury and increase members' purchasing power by enabling them to borrow money at low interest rates. The interest paid on loans, by borrowers, pays the dividends on shares, and the running costs of the union. As a union expands, these costs include the hiring of a part- or full-time treasurer;
- to train and educate members in business methods and self-government, and to help them realise the value of mutual co-operation and mutual aid.

There is a myth that credit unions cannot work because the people who most need them are incapable of running them. But statistics contradict this. Between 1979 and 1985:

- the number of credit unions grew from 55 to 64;
- the numbers of adult members grew from 8,500 to 17,727;
- the total assets grew from £850,000 to £3,691,646;
- the average value of £1 shares per member rose from £95 to £186.

Add the fact, as I said earlier, that the bad debt rate is less than a quarter that of ordinary banks, and it hardly adds up to incompetence. This is to say nothing of the number of working men's clubs and trade unions run by people with no professional or management experience or training, very successfully.

So we are back to one important principle which I went into in an earlier chapter—that activities like this have enormous potential for our own learning and development, and so are worth working at and attempting for what they teach us, if for no other reason. Credit unions have done much to educate in their social, economic, democratic and self-help principles, as well as in the rights and responsibilities of members.

Conclusion

At the heart of credit unions is the principle of human development and the brotherhood of man, expressed through people working together to achieve a better life for themselves and their community. Members' voting rights are not dependent upon the amount of savings or deposits, and elected officers to not receive salaries. Any surplus belongs to and benefits all members.

We belong to a society in which making more money has become an end in itself, and where the most money is made from those who can least afford it. The message from money lenders is a highly tempting one: 'Let us clear up all your debts with one big easy loan.' Time and again, borrowers start off with several small debts of a few hundred pounds, and swap them for one big one. They finish up with several such loans, totalling literally thousands of pounds. When they cannot pay, they are usually treated as criminals, while those who have encouraged them are considered legitimate.

Logically, one might expect those who extol 'Victorian values' and low inflation to be thoroughly in favour of organisations committed to promoting thrift and savings, and more competent use of money. Just the opposite—there has never been less encouragement to save. Not only are savers penalised by the DHSS when applying for benefits, but tax exemption on dividends paid to credit union savers was ended in March 1985. Even so, credit unions are growing in popularity, both in this country and worldwide, including Ireland, Australia, Canada and the USA.

So now there is potential for an alternative merry-go-round which looks like this:

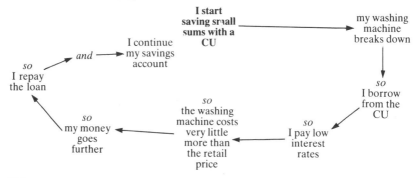

120

If you want more details about credit unions you can get them from your local Co-operative Development Office, or by writing to:

The Credit Union League of Great Britain,
Ecumenical Centre,
Firbeck, Skelmersdale,
Lancashire, WN8 6PN

—to whom go my thanks for much of the factual material in this section.

9 Up to Your Neck in it

Introduction

If you are setting out on the sort of journey this book is meant to encourage—to help yourself and to work with others who have been made redundant or perhaps have never had a job—it is essential to know something of the process which most people seem to have to go through before they can even begin to think constructively.

If you don't understand sympathetically, not only how others feel, but what you might be into yourself, you may be frustrated when others are not ready to share your vision and travel with you, or when you yourself cannot work up the energy to do much. You may wonder, 'Am I normal? Perhaps I'm going mad. I can't see any hope of getting better.'

You may not be able to give others the support you would like to give, through not understanding their problems. Well-meaning but ill-informed 'helpers' can often make matters worse.

In this chapter I shall look at how unemployment and redundancy affects both the people immediately hit and their families, in terms of physical illness and stress. I shall try to show what sort of help or response from others might be appropriate at each stage. I shall also look at the way that some people have managed to turn what was initially a disaster into a positive turning point in their lives.

Oh God, Help me!
So wrote a redundant manager in a foot-note to a letter to me

a few years back. Thousands of others feel like this and would be able to say with complete conviction the words of someone up to his neck in it 3,000 years ago:

Save me O God
    The water is up to my neck,
I am sinking in deep mud
    and there is no solid ground;
I am out in deep water,
    and the waves are about to drown me;
I am worn out from calling for help,
    and my throat is achng;
I have strained my eyes,
    looking for your help.*

Let's face it, redundancy seldom gives much cause for joy, even if the financial compensation is generous. But does it have to be destructive? Certainly, it is not easy to cope with in its earliest stages, however many times it has happened before, and even if you see it coming. There are seldom any short cuts to this stage. Later I shall quote from some people who have found ways of coping. Some have even found the experience liberating in a way they never thought possible.

The path

I know from my own experience of being made redundant, that although in my head I understood much of the process, that did not prevent or reduce the pain and anger I felt when it happened. I am convinced that there is some kind of progress for most people along the lines I describe here, but these stages are not solid stepping stones. And although the general direction is there,

---

*Psalm 69: vv 1–3, *Good News Bible,* published by The Bible Societies, Collins/Fontana. It is worth reading the whole Psalm. It could have been written by a redundant worker up to his eyes in unpaid bills and H.P. payments, surrounded by an uncaring society, loaded with feelings of guilt, inadequacy and isolation from friends and enemies alike. But in the end, after pouring his heart out, the spirit of hope comes through even when there is no cause for optimism.

people usually find themselves straddling two or three stages at once. Experience of loss is personal, and affects each individual differently, depending on social and environmental factors. Then, of course, some people are re-employed fairly quickly, others never are.

However, I have found this stepping stones description useful myself in counselling redundant people, and I have also experienced most of the stages myself.

Redundancy

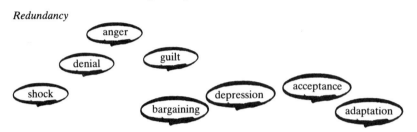

Grief is obviously a symptom of loss. It varies in intensity according to the significance of the job lost. But the first reaction is usually a sense of *shock*, generally accompanied by *denial*. The shock can be almost anaesthetic (physically and mentally), keeping everything around us at a distance, and with an unreal quality. I have heard it described as 'surrounded by cotton wool'. This is not necessarily unhealthy; it is often a help to keep our loss at a distance while we adjust.

Along with the shock we may well react also by *denying* that anything is happening. 'Oh, no!', 'I don't believe it', or 'It's only a temporary set-back. I won't have any difficulty finding something else with my experience'. We very often use such means to set up a mental barrier against absorbing our awareness of the shock. Sometimes a group of people may work together, if they are in the same boat, to try to persuade their employers to change their minds about a closure or redundancies. They may even succeed.

But in most cases, when eventually reality does creep in, or the reversal attempt fails, a mixture of different emotions can flood in, including:

Anger   'Why pick on me?' 'How dare they do this after all I've done.' 'How incompetent and useless this firm is!' But this wish to see the problem as someone else's fault may also turn inwards and become—

Guilt   'I should have seen this coming.' 'If I had made a better effort on that contract.' 'I could have avoided this.' We may chew over in our minds time and again different things we have said or done to people, or actions we have taken which may have contributed to the disaster or soured a relationship along the line. In the process we may begin a process of—

Bargaining   in which we fantasise about how we might have done things differently, how things could have been better—a job improved, or an issue or problem resolved. But when we get to this stage, it is usually a sign of reaching the final stage of letting go of the past, and we frequently find ourselves in a stage of—

Depression   which accompanies the ultimate acceptance of the reality that 'it has happened to me'. We may and do feel pain, or rejection, sometimes fear and general dejection and grief. We may break into tears unexpectedly (no bad thing) and withdraw into ourselves, Our moods come and go in intensity, like waves, depending on circumstances around us.

These are stages we have to work through, and often only time makes much difference, although I shall show later how some people find that having a structure to their day and making motions which are actions 'as if' they felt some sense of purpose when they do not have any, do seem to move them forward. What does not seem to help, at least in the early stages, is people telling us to 'pull yourself together'.

There are a very few cases where people have never been able to *accept* their loss. But the majority of us do come to the position where we are able to ask, 'How do I cope with this new state?' We stop blaming ourselves or other people, and begin to look elsewhere for purpose and contacts. At first this usually means applying for a job in the trade or field previously engaged in. But just as a man or woman has to work out how to be a divorcee, widow or widower (instead of wife or husband) if his/her spouse dies, so steel workers, for example, may have to come to the conclusion that they can no longer present themselves under this label, and *adapt* by doing one or two things depending upon their age. Either:

- apply for re-training in a completely new area of work—e.g. become a computer programmer or hairdresser—or at least apply for jobs in trades other than steel (or become self-employed); or

- adjust to being of unemployed status, and start finding a purpose and meaning to life, engaging in activities and relationships which assume there will be no traditional full-time work for some time. It may still be necessary to go through the motions to obtain benefits by calling in at the Job Centre weekly.

This second adjustment is often the hardest, but need not mean that we have opted out of wanting to work. It may be the only way in which we can retain our self-respect until work becomes available.

If, like me, you can follow theories more easily when they are related to actual people and events, you will find the following a fairly accurate reflection of all that I have written so far in this chapter.

THE BURN NEWSLETTER

No. 2   NEWSLETTER OF THE BRITISH UNEMPLOYMENT RESOURCE NETWORK   March 1983

TO ESCAPE THE NIGHTMARE
~One man's story

I had never known such Misery; it was two weeks before Christmas; I was driving home from a weeks work for the last time. Hours before, with no warning, I was told I was no longer required and in lieu of notice I was to be paid up to two months; I would be paid but I need never return to work.

There was shame even in that. I loved my job; we had planned to move and the house was for sale – to be nearer my work. We had a buyer and had found a small but very beautiful cottage. I was over-stretched but until now there seemed only one way and that was up. I was always being praised for my work and effort; my boss was a personal friend yet he had shown no personal regret. Only two days before, we had been planning operations over the Christmas holiday. It must have been a drumhead decision.

I reached a small village before my climb over the Pennine Moors. It was dusk, the cottage lights twinkled and Xmas trees had been erected here and there. A light covering of snow had fallen. Twinkling jewels on black velvet sprinkled with sugar. Suddenly the pent up emotions were released. Shock, bitterness, self-pity, despair. In the middle of the village, I stopped, no longer able to see, crying as I had never cried, overwhelmed by sheer hopelessness. The employment position was well know, I was turned 40, limited qualifications. Jumbles flew through my mind, debt, eviction, bailiffs, county court, bankruptcy, shame, the pity of friends, the scorn of associates. I noticed the curious looks of passers by and drove on, following the steep, dangerous Pennine lanes. Again and again I was taken by an urge to steer the car into a ravine and escape the nightmare, but somehow I reached home.

> ## "Suddenly the pent-up emotions were released. Shock, bitterness, self-pity, despair."

I don't remember much of the next few weeks, except to say of it as a sea of mounting bills, threats from creditors, monotinous repeated unconvincing excuses from Government for my plight and thousands of others, poor meals, no social life, raggier clothes, rows and my wife becoming a drudge. The indifference, nay aggressiveness of the Social Security making me feel a criminal. County Court, bailiffs at the door, all I'd worked for disappearing before my eyes and all the time Thatcher's platitudes, excuses and unfulfilled promises. Overall, a total feeling of helplessness.

> ## "For myself, I learned that far from being redundant, I was needed as never before. To help create a different world and not accept what it had become."

Then one day, I saw an advert for an unemployment group. No details, just come and see us. I did. They met in the upper room of the local swimming baths. Men from all walks of life, and women, angry, bitter, frustrated, yet determined to take some action. But what? We had no guidelines, no experience, no real idea what we should do. I could go on at length about the arguments, the opinions, the casting around but there isn't room. Suffice to say that ideas gradually became reality. Advice service, debt councelling, pressure on creditors, Social Security, tribunals. Leisure creation, personal problems, education, work creation, co-operatives, voluntary work. It seemed endless, yet eventually it all began to co-ordinate.

Most important, I had something to do. I was wanted, needed and no longer facing the world and its problems alone. It sounds melodramatic, but it was true.

Quite early on I spotted an advert for a Job Change Conference in Birmingham and attended on the Group's behalf. It was here I realised that many other groups were forming independently. A national picture was beginning to emerge. Much has been and will be written about Birmingham Settlement, its unsinkable Director, Peter Houghton and Willie More, Andrew Howell and their staff on Job Change Project; possible pioneers of a new way of life? Why not. No-one deserves it more.

For myself, I learned that far from being redundant, I was needed as never before. To help create a different world and not accept what it had become. The conference expressed so much, I could not find space to record it and it has been written elsewhere (contact Andrew Howell, c/o BURN).

I decided, through the inspiration I received, to devote most of my time to work creation. I took the attitude that whoever's fault the situation was, bleating and protesting would not change it. Creativitiy would. I set up a co-operative for unemployed offenders, an adventurous scheme encouraged by the staff of Birmingham and patiently guided by dear old Ken Smart of Associated Resources, another Job Change venture (See Issue 1 of The BURN Newsletter -'Something Fishy'). Because of my persistent contact with the Probation Service and the Adult Education Authority, I received frequent contracts to teach and supervise. On the invitation of the Job Change Project I became a member of the BURN Steering Committee and had opportunity to travel, meet people and negotiate and discuss at high level, their part in the country's future.

People listened, they helped and what was most important to me was that I mattered, I was wanted, I was needed. I had a position in society after all.

The men of the Settlement were shrewd. They had studied and worked towards all the possible roads for a national answer, but most important they recognised a man's needs for his own self respect, his need to be a member of society, for some purpose. I am forever in their debt.

Now, all my time is occupied in some direction. Helping others like I was advising, guiding, creating, teaching and loving every minute. Yes, I'm still not totally employed, but I'm managing and I matter. I know I have something to give, to contribute. As long as people will get together and work to find an answer, they will find what they seek. It's hard work. I think of John Appleyard and his burning of midnight oil, not on his own behalf but on behalf of people he hasn't met yet. Willie More and the appalling risks he takes so that his ideas will survive. Guy Dauncey, writing his inspiring advice that but for unemployment would never have been written. Peter Houghton, to whom people matter before all theories, economics, politics and personal gain, and hundreds of others I have met, who I could only mention by making a list on a roll of wallpaper. So, there is no need to sit down and drown in regret and self-pity. Get up, join in and live again. I did. You Will.

Tony Ledward
90 Blackburn Drive,
Barncross, Sheffield

Half way house

For most people redundancy is a major trauma, and it is unhelpful to suggest that it is not so for those involved and their families. But it does not have to mean the end of living. It *does* mean taking advice about reorganising finances at an early stage, and this often has to be done when the shock and despair are at their worst, before the bills get too big (just as it has to be done by a widow at the worst time in her life).

Many people have found that they have not only adapted, they have actually enriched their lives or become more independent since redundancy in a way they would never have thought possible. I have tried to illustrate this in this book.

However, while going through shock and grief, and anger and so on, we do need friends or other supporters who will listen patiently, and just accept us as going through a bad patch, 'through a phase and not a conclusion', and not just try to get us 'to snap out of it', or try to give unwanted advice.

> The main thing I learned from my redundancy was that never again will I let myself be totally dependent on other people for my income, my interests in life or how I live my life.
>
> Redundant engineer

Effects on health

The effects of job loss are often not only psychological, but also physical. I have heard of marathon runners who on being made redundant expected to be able to spend more time training; after a month or two they were only able to run a few miles. I have seen others visibly shrink, staying at home, in extreme cases hardly able to walk a dog after a year. The psychologists say this is a way of substituting the lost label of 'working man' with that of 'sick man'—for we believe it is more acceptable to society to be sick than to be 'unemployed'.

A study of 1,000 unemployed men 6 months after a steel plant closure in 1976* showed anxiety, depression, listlessness, insomnia, lack of confidence, irritability, inability to concentrate and

---

*Peter Warr, "Work, Jobs and Unemployment"—Psychological Society Bulletin 1983

general nervousness. However, the reverse is also true. Some people's health actually *improves* once they are freed from the stresses of their job.

Where single or other women are the principal wage earners, the effect of redundancy on them seems to be the same as it is on men. But having young children seems to make a difference—a lot of women do not depend on a job to feel good about themselves, say the researchers. (The main exception to this is working class mothers, contrary to popular belief.)

People who already have health problems, such as heart trouble, arthritis, back problems and so on, certainly seem to suffer more the longer unemployment goes on.

Effects on family health

What we do know is that in our concern for the person who actually loses the job, we often overlook the effects of the loss on their nearest and dearest. Not only men, but their spouses experience recurrent disorders such as asthma, insomnia, headaches and gastro-intestinal complaints (if they had previous experience of these), and almost all suffer some depression.*

Job loss by the breadwinner also affects the children. They often feel neglected when parents, not unnaturally, feel entirely 'taken over' by their experience and worries, spending hours talking to each other or absorbed in their private grief.

Problems at school

Many children whose parents are made redundant deteriorate in their school work and perhaps play truant. They may steal when they do not normally, or become more infantile or demanding in their behaviour. Some have to be taken to their doctor because they refuse to eat, have tummy upsets or earache and are generally unmanageable.

Children's health depends a lot on the relationship between their parents. A trauma such as redundancy can cause male impotence and female frigidity; the parents may even be driven

---

*Studies by Dr. Leonard Fagin, recorded in the RCP Bulletin—quoted by Dr. Frank Lake, Clinical Theology Newsletter No. 39, December 1981.

towards separation, so the children are bound to suffer. Many unemployed people are completely unaware of the possible effects the loss of their job can have on their families (or even on themselves). Being aware of the possible effects and preparing for them can lessen the severity of the effects and long-term damage to self-confidence and self-esteem.

Effects on young people

For teenagers, the main effect of being unemployed is loss of self-esteem and lack of any identity to help them move into the adult world. If you have never had a job, you cannot even call yourself a redundant worker/brick-layer/plasterer. Youth training schemes act as a buffer, and do alleviate some of the effects of unemployment on the young. They may go back to their former state if they fail to obtain a job at the end of their training, but they probably won't be any worse than they were before the scheme.

Relationships

Just as adults' relationships are affected by unemployment (whether with their spouse, friends, children, or others in society), so are teenagers'. Their normal progression of relationships is upset, at a time when they would hope and expect to be moving into a more adult and responsible phase in their lives.

With employed friends

It is not uncommon for unemployed youngsters to lose status and therefore the friendship of former school friends. They are thrown back on to groups of other unemployed youngsters, and perhaps to those still at school whom they might otherwise not see much.

On the other hand, a strong group of unemployed teenagers might put pressure on to employed friends to leave their jobs to be more acceptable in the group. By the same process, if a group decide they want to get work, they have been known to find jobs more quickly than would otherwise be the case, even when there is competition.

With parents

It can cause a lot of strain to have an unemployed teenager hanging around all day, with very little money and not much interest in life. Parents need to be more loving and tolerant than at any other time. This is especially true if neither parent has been through the problem of jobless living, and cannot understand the effect it can have. Families have been known to be split up by the teenager moving out.

With the opposite sex

It seems that a much higher proportion of employed youngsters are either engaged or have had a long-standing relationship with a member of the opposite sex than those not employed. Boys seem to find it harder than girls to start courting regularly whilst unemployed, feeling like 'non-people' because of the lack of a job.*

With police

A higher proportion of unemployed youngsters become involved in criminal activity than those with jobs. This is probably only partly due to the search for extra cash; criminal activity can be just as much a form of work to some as a traditional job. Unemployed youngsters are also more at risk because they have more opportunity to associate with others with criminal tendencies. Most of those carrying out criminal activities stop them as soon as they land a job, but it is hard to show them how a thoughtless act at the age of 17–18 can effect their chances when applying for something more responsible later on.

Enough doom and gloom

Of course the negative effects of redundancy and unemployment

---

*I am indebted to Michael Gillingham for much of this material, taken from his 'Enquiry into the Effects of Unemployment on Young People, with reference to their inter-personal relationships' for the Diploma in Social and Community Education, University College of Swansea, 1983.

are terrible. But it's not all despair. As I said earlier, some people have found life much better since stopping work, because their job was stressful or was done in awful conditions. Others have said 'enough is enough', and left work even though they could not see any other job prospect.

The popular picture of the unemployed male is of someone staying in bed until midday because there is nothing to get up for, who then hangs around the house suffering from depression and getting on the family's nerves. This may be true of some men, but certainly not of all. Quite a lot of unemployed people go to bed early to save on heating and lighting, perhaps watching T.V., and I have myself seen men in areas where males do not traditionally have much to do with household chores or children, washing nappies, cleaning the house, working and playing with their children.

Some adopt unique life styles, such as a man in Newcastle who turned night into day by rising at 4.00 p.m. and, after doing some housework, spends most of the night reading, going through the sort of non-fiction he had no time for when he was working. His wife works a day shift.

Ground rules

Of all the comments and writing I have come across on unemployment I found the following to be the most generally relevant and practical for those who do not have many options, either because they have limited interests or limited income. I first came across it in a parish church magazine in Letchworth, which had it from the Anglican Healing Centre in Crowhurst. The author lives in Battersea. I reproduce it here because it seems to me to show how someone has found hope for himself by a wilful act of ordering his daily life.

EXPERIENCING UNEMPLOYMENT

by Julian Francis

For six months I have been collecting unemployment benefit. On occasions I have felt, or been made to feel, guilty. It is disturbing how deeply common prejudice is against you. However, I have not felt unemployed. I have not experienced the time as long, idle days with nothing to do, nowhere to go, and no one to be with. In fact it would be a glaring misrepresentation to attach the lable 'unemployment'. It has been, rather, an adventure of living in an unstructured way. But it has only been possible by virtue of living in a house with six friends. Had I been living alone with few friends close by, I am quite sure that I would by now be in decay. That I have lived, and not decayed has been my good fortune. It is common to hear of unemployment as 'going to seed'. It is sadly the rule. It has not been my lot, however.

I was faced, then, by whole days stretching open in front of me. It would appear that there is nothing obvious to do in such a situation, and no obvious way in which to do it! But I came to realise that there are certain basic ingredients in such a day, and here are some of them:

1. **A day requires that I get up.** It is easy to get up when there's the 7.50 a.m. train to catch to take me to my place of work. However, there is less reason to get up at week-ends, still less on holiday. How often is it said "If I've got time off I stay in bed". But for the most part, the natural inclination is to get up early. It is a matter of habit. For the unemployed person, especially the young unemployed, getting up is a battle. I spoke to a young man recently who told me he never got up before 11 a.m. What was the point, he asked? This is the crux of the matter. If there's no job to go to, what is there to get up for? And what kind of a day is left over when the morning is spent in bed or indoors? A lethargic start means a lethargic day. I once heard it said that the first step to heaven is to buy an alarm clock. The alarm clock is an indispensable resource, particularly for the unemployed. It enables the first obstacle on the course to be overcome. Regularity in getting up is the first step towards an ordered life.

2. **To be clean and tidy is a second early morning requirement.** It is a simple but profound truth that exterior tidiness encourages interior stability. If I am clean and well dressed, and my surroundings are in good order, I feel happier in myself. Inner decay very quickly sets in and establishes itself when I am shabby and my environment is in chaos.

   These first two ingredients pave the way for a day. If I don't muster the resolve to get up when the alarm goes, and to keep myself and my surroundings clean and tidy, I am unlikely to have the inclination to do anything, least of all anything creative or purposeful. Given these 'starters' what is there to do?

3. **Food must be prepared.** It is the 'chips and chocolate' syndrome that is the scourge of unstructured living. Giving time, energy and consideration to preparation of food is important. It is both a creative use of time, and a valuable exercise in itself. Eating is about refreshment, not just mastication and digestion. The art of cooking and eating is one that those with extra time on their hands would do well to cultivate. They would be doing it not only for themselves.

4. **Fresh air must be had daily.** It would be a revealing statistic, were the number of people who get no fresh air between dawn and dusk to be calculated. (I was alarmed to read recently that 1 in 5 young mothers don't venture out of their homes during the day). Too many hours are spent in the stale air. And again, stale air leads to inner staleness. A walk to the shops, a bicycle journey, a stroll in the park, a trip out with the dog, even a run—one such must be on the day's agenda.

5. **There is a need to see faces.** There is a need to see faces to whom we belong. These may be the friends who share our house or flat—the family we are part of—or an animal that shares our life. But we also need to be aware of our membership of the wider community. To be on the "Underground" or in a crowded bus, or in a supermarket, provides an awareness of belonging to this larger community. It is not something of which we are consciously aware, perhaps, but it is an important experience. It is a foil to home-bound isolation.

6. **There is a need to be creative.** The needs for fulfilment and satisfaction are in question here. They are needs not readily met in any sphere of living, and for many unemployed people the meeting of these needs is almost in the realms of fantasy. To be creative with mind or hands, in reading, studying, gardening, painting, etc. is an option for only some people. Many have neither the necessary skill nor the inclination to do any of these. Nor are the facilities or opportunity very often available. Not least, of course, they are all pastimes that cost money. Money that is not there!

A day's activity requires planning. The plan is the very element already present in a job-based day, but that is missing altogether in a "jobless" day. There is no ready-made structure. This can to an extent be overcome by the setting of objectives. This is the cementing factor for a day's activities. The objectives must be clear, set out on paper, reasonable to the time available, and physically and emotionally attainable. The latter is very important. For it is achievement that is so vital to self-esteem. Objectives must be set in line with achievable goals. There is however one important assumption being made—that a person has the motivation to set objectives at all—or even to address themselves to their situation. When the basis of living has been taken away, what is there to live for? It is clear that the whole matter of motivation needs to be thoroughly looked into. I do not intend to offer any suggestions, but it has been my experience that motivation is fuelled by the doing of some of the six ingredients outlined above. It is my principle suggestion that some dignity can be salvaged through the learning and living of a day's basic activities.

Julian's experience and discoveries will be echoed by many elderly folk. When I was younger, I often wondered why so many retired people went to so much trouble to dress up every day. With the arrogance of youth we used to speak of them 'trying to think they're still important—something in the City'. Now, of course, I realise they *are* still important, have learned self-respect, and have found the creative value of structure in their lives.

Conclusion

Prevention *is* better than cure. It can be helpful to know that certain things might happen, and that you are not alone and do not feel any differently from hundreds of other people in the same boat.

For the unemployed or redundant person, the sympathy of others is not enough. And if you are in any way involved with unemployed people, it can relieve you and them of tremendous fears and anxieties if you understand what they may be experiencing. It helps to know what to expect if you are married to someone who loses their job, or if you have a teenager leaving school without a job, or losing their job. It helps to know that your smaller child's irrational behaviour, or the stomach cramps experienced by your spouse in the middle of the night, are not sure signs either of budding delinquency or of malignant disease.

To understand these things and to react appropriately is not just for professional 'carers'. The unemployed are not a separate species of humanity—we are part of them and they of us. In being with them and helping them we are helping ourselves and they are enriching us. It is neither an altruistic exercise for us, nor need it be a humiliation for them.

136

■10 Get it Together

The more we are together . . . the more we fight!

I have already mentioned one unfortunate fact of life. That is, although a group of people may get together full of idealism and a desire to do something worthwhile for themselves, their group or the community they live in, within a few months many will drop out. Those who are left may be beset by internal squabbles and external criticisms. The fun and excitement have gone out of the project, and even if progress is marked by opening a building, the occasion is notable as much for those who stay away as for those who turn out.

In this chapter I shall look at some of the common reasons for this, and suggest ways of overcoming the problems—ways which have been well tried and tested in a variety of settings. One or two I have already covered and will refer back to.

What goes wrong?

It is always a useful exercise to ask a group involved in a project to sit down in twos or threes with a piece of paper and a pen, and to list the problems they have working with other people. They usually come up with a list something like this:

- too little information flowing from the top or people in key positions
- too much information flowing from the top or people in key positions

- duplication of effort
- important work not done
- decisions made without consultation
- all consultation but no decisions
- endless meetings
- high-handed autocratic attitudes
- off-hand laissez-faire attitudes by people at top
- biased chairmanship
- badly organised or poorly chaired meetings
- people not listening to each other
- last minute panic for everything
- minutes lost or arriving too late
- agreed action not taken
- everyone expects someone else to do things
- some people overloaded with jobs
- some people with nothing or not enough to do
- new people do not fit in or feel left out
- people feel unsupported
- rivalry between paid staff and volunteers
- rivalry or ill-feeling between men and women
- ill feeling between ethnic groups
- too tight a financial control system, meanness
- lack of financial controls
- too much paper work
- no imagination shown
- secretive management
- poor co-operation
- too many people waiting for somebody else's orders
- too many people taking initiatives
- all activity, but no discussion on where we are going
- all discussion but no activity
- field workers feel too remote
- interference by others in your work
- lack of interest by others in your work
- people do not get on with each other
- too many new innovations.

You could probably add at least as many examples of your own to this list. But you will see that it includes most of the more common problems. If you look carefully, most of the problems fall into several fundamental categories.

Structures

It is no coincidence that in large organisations the most senior people occupy the top floor of the building. This is symbolic of our thinking about organisations. Similarly, when we draw pictures of organisations we draw them in ladder-type boxes, the most senior at the top. If there is a voluntary management body, that goes at the top too. This is how such a drawing generally looks:

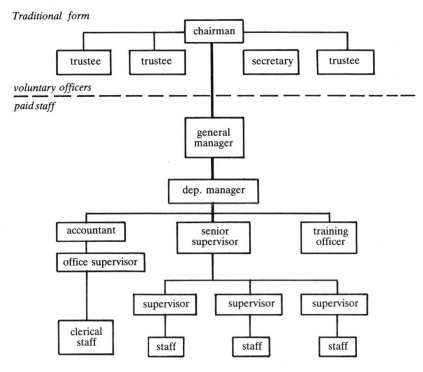

Traditional form

voluntary officers

paid staff

This sort of picture does not really show what is happening. Also, the organisation may have been set up with ideals or norms which are opposed to traditional hierarchies. It may be looking for a more egalitarian way of working, trying to free itself of the old ways of 'top dog' versus 'underdog'. The sort of chart in the drawing is static and keeps people thinking along traditional organisational lines. And it does not include any relationships with its customers or clients, or with the community.

The organisation as a system

Another way to look at an organisation is to see it as an organic system, where each part has its own functions. In a diagram it would look like this:

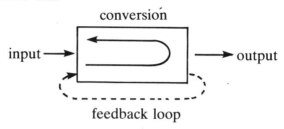

This assumes that the whole organisation exists to convert whatever is put into it into something else. If it is a car factory it exists to convert the parts into complete vehicles. If it is a social service it exists to convert problem families into coping or healthy families. Each part of the organisation is a cell which has the same function, taking in and giving out.

For example, a community programme set up to provide work decorating pensioners' homes, doing community care work and running a community print shop, could be drawn like this:

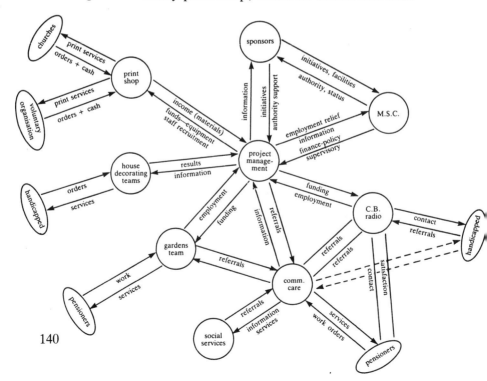

This is a more dynamic way of looking at what is going on, and it moves people away from thinking in terms of top or bottom status. It is also a useful way for each part of a group to work out what it is giving and receiving. The 'feedback loop' is an important part of the process. An organisation needs to receive information from other parties, such as its customers, suppliers, or the community, as a result of which it may have to revise its operations.

Stages of development

A common problem for many new organisations, whether business entrepreneurs or social initiatives, is when they start to grow and go through a crisis in their development. This crisis occurs when the key figure, who in the early stages does almost everything, can no longer cope and has to employ specialists— accountants, marketing managers, office managers, engineers and so on.

The problems arise if the initiator is still trying to run the project as he/she did at the start, making all the decisions, knowing everybody and speaking to them all daily, and probably working long hours. The initiator often finds it difficult to let go of the reins and delegate, so the accountant or engineer cannot operate without interference, and other people who have worked with the initiator from the start resent the fact that they now have to go through someone else, and do not get to see 'the boss' direct every day.

In such a case, the initiator gets more and more bogged down in detail. Some jobs get duplicated, others are left undone, decisions are contradicted or not taken at all. Staff play off one against another or become demoralised, and the quality of work or service suffers.

This is the sort of situation where an outsider experienced in working out an operational system can be very useful. Remember you are not unique! Lots of organisations have this sort of problem after the first flush of growth.

Management style

This term is used frequently to describe how an organisation is run. There are all sorts of ways of describing style—the simplest are these three:

Autocratic—what the boss says goes. It may be done with a certain amount of benevolent paternalism or with flair, but it is still the same thing and does not allow for much participation except by permission of the boss;

Democratic—this can mean a whole range of letting go of authority, from consulting staff *before* making important decisions, even allowing them to outvote the manager, to the state where the manager, having made his/her own mind up already, seeks advice as to how to carry out his/her decisions;

Laissez-faire—this is almost management by opting out: the manager lets people get on with things the way they want to, and is not really interested in what they are doing or how they do it.

A case can be made for and against each of the above, depending on the task and the situation. The important thing is to know which style you want your project to operate under and work towards it. These things do not just happen, they have to be planned and worked at. And they are not fixed: sometimes people need help to change to a more participative way of managing, especially when they have worked only in organisations run along traditional lines. They may find themselves carrying on in a way they despised in other people when they were employed under them. We shall look at how to get help later.

A common reason for disputes in voluntary or other organisations with social objectives is the way decisions are made. People in charge often believe they have *consulted* others, and say they have, when in fact what they have done is *informed* them. Consultation happens *before* a decision is taken, when it is possible for those consulted to influence the decision. If discussion happens *after* the decision is taken, then it is *information*, although the decision-maker may still be open to influence on its implementation.

It may be *quicker* to inform than consult, but those involved are usually more committed to making a decision work if they are consulted first, and can see their influence on the decision. Also, they will often take more risks together than they would alone. Remember—the best decisions can be blocked by people determined enough not to implement them.

Collectivity

Some organisations manage to set up collective ways of working, with no managers or director, or to set collective terms within a larger body. This is not easy; there is no one formula or pattern, and other staff, outside bodies, and funding agencies don't find it easy to cope with since nobody seems to be accountable.

For more information on this, with examples of people who have tried it successfully, contact:

The Management Development Unit,
NCVO,
26 Bedford Square, London WC1B 3HU

and ask for Bulletin 3/4 of July 1984.

Goals or objectives – where are we heading?

In Chapter 2, I pointed out that there will be problems in any group if those working on a project together have different views as to why the organisation exists, and how its aims should be achieved. I also described ways in which these problems could be tackled. There is no point in repeating myself here. But 'What are we trying to do, what is our primary task?' is a key question well worth asking ourselves from time to time.

Working out agreed objectives is difficult enough, but is no use unless people actually follow them. You need some sort of monitoring mechanism, otherwise groups or individuals may stray from the objectives, sometimes not even realizing they have done so.

Who does what around here?

Whether the people involved are paid or working voluntarily, makes little difference; there are a number of ways in which they can fall short of each others' expectations. Two people may do exactly the same job, but:

- one may prefer the paper work, the other prefers to be out and about;
- one may be a good time keeper, the other frequently turns up late, or sends in his returns or reports late;

- one may deluge other people with letters and memos, the other prefers to use the telephone and hardly writes at all;
- one may share out work among colleagues or subordinates, the other tries to do it all;
- one may hold frequent meetings with others, the other says very little to anyone;

and so on.

When we are involved in doing things with other people, a network of expectations builds up:

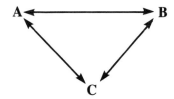

A, B, and C each have expectations of each other, e.g.:

A may expect B to do certain things that B may not think are his job;

B may expect to do other things that C thought were her tasks;

C gets upset with A because he never gives her the information or time she needs to plan her job.

There are a number of ways in which you can resolve these issues:

- each person could complain to someone else—perhaps their superior, or go home and complain to the family;
- they could go to the other and complain along the lines of, 'why the hell don't you . . ?'
- they could approach the problem in a mature way, using a simple basic discipline which starts off as a written exercise but becomes a more informal way once people are familiar with it. It is one of the most useful 'tools' for helping relationships I have come across.

The basic discipline consists of each person in the group, team or pair, thinking about how the other(s) operate, what they do which helps or hinders their own work, and how it does so. They then make out a sheet of paper for each person, under three headings:

```
From:                     To:
1.  Things I would like you to do more of, and why:        (more of)


    Response

2.  Things I would like you to continue doing, and why:    (the same)


    Response

3.  Things I would like you to do less of, and why:        (less of)


    Response
```

If there are four people working in a team, each person will write up three sheets. When each person has done this for each of the others, they give the sheets to each other. Then they sit with each one in turn to work through the sheets, both exchanging the 'more of' requests first, then the 'same as', and finally the 'less of'.

When each person receives a sheet from another the possible responses could be:

Yes, I agree with that and will co-operate.
No, I see no reason for that, or, it is not possible, and why.
It might be possible if you were to help me with . . . or by . . .

It is often useful to have a third party listening in, especially if a pair get bogged down.

When a pair reaches agreement, each person writes out what is agreed and both sign it. They include a date for checking that what they agree is actually happening, and a mechanism for feedback if something is going wrong.

Notice the following features of this method:

- The exercise is *not* just for criticising, it also enables appreciation of things the other person is doing well (same as). It is important *not* to fill in just one of the sections, but to attempt all three.

- There are two parts under each heading. The first part

describes what you want changed, *or* continued. The second part says what difference this will make. This prevents carping criticism—you are not just saying you don't like something, but showing how a change will make a difference to you. If it won't make any difference to you, it is probably better to let the others do things their own way!

- Putting your request down on paper 'defuses' it emotionally, both for you and the recipient.

- The requests may not be just about the actual work, they can also be about behaviour, e.g. embarrassing habits, irritating or offensive phrases or comments which you or customers/visitors feel reflect badly on the rest.

- A pair may need to consult someone else before concluding an agreement, if their agreement will affect them.

This structure has been used very successfully in marriage guidance. Partly it reduces the emotional level; partly, once people have done it a few times, they find it easier to say to each other, 'Can we sit down a moment and work something out?', and keep their cool while working at it, often without having to write it down at all.

> The secretary of an organisation filled out a sheet to the treasurer, asking for certain figures to be supplied on time each month, and not 2 weeks late, so that the secretary could compile his own statistics.
>
> After discussing the amount of work which the treasurer felt was not strictly necessary, they consulted the rest of the management group who agreed that a quarterly return would be quite adequate. The secretary and treasurer signed an agreement whereby the treasurer agreed to supply the figures by the 7th of the month following each quarter, and set time afterwards to discuss whether the date was feasible or needed adjusting.

There is more detailed explanation of this and other approaches to team work in *Task Oriented Team Development* Irwin M. Rubin *et al.* (McGraw-Hill, 1978).

The full-time worker – who loves yer, baby?

What excitement! A group deeply committed to their cause, who have slaved for months, argued their case in endless council committee meetings, produced reams of budgets and revised budgets, written dozens of applications for help to charities and trusts, at last have sufficient funding to employ a field worker, full- or part-time. The job description is drawn up (with many a laugh at the likelihood of locating a wonder woman or superman to fit the job!); it is advertised, the interviews are carefully carried out, and the appointment is made. The management group breathes a sigh of relief, and the secretary and others thankfully hand over the files and details of 'Work in Progress'. 'Just give us a call if you want to know anything', they say, 'you'll soon get into the swing of it.'

But will he or she? Even if the job description is precise, which it frequently is not, there is a mountain of information the worker needs to know, most of which is not written down, contacts that volunteers have made over the previous months. The lady who was happy to type voluntarily for Jim the secretary has a very decided reluctance to do the same thing for Jeanette the worker. The chairperson has a very clear idea that the worker's priority should be getting the administration straight, whereas the treasurer feels he/she should spend a lot of time at first building up contacts. The management group are surprised to find that their new worker, who seemed well experienced, has never had to contact local authority officials, and feels very ill-equipped. Soon, the new worker is clearly unhappy, feeling under tremendous pressure to solve the group's problems and show results, but at the same time isolated and enslaved.

This is a very common problem. We tend to forget all the processes we have been through, the contacts we have made, and the fact that we had a particular reason for doing something, or doing it in a particular way which the field worker will not know.

Induction

There are some basic activities which the management group can carry out to help the field worker get going in the job, and not feel that everything has been unloaded by others:

- Each member of the management group can write down a list headed *Things it will be helpful to know*, including people involved, telephone numbers, short histories. There will be some overlap by different members, but this will not matter.

- A small group from the management committee needs to sit down before the worker starts and make sure the group has a clear policy statement.

- When the worker begins this same group needs to meet him or her regularly and agree priorities, realistic targets and what tasks are to be carried out.

- This group may conclude that some particular knowledge or skill which the worker does not have will be best provided by sending the worker on a short course of training. Management groups who are not very experienced in recruiting are often surprised to find that their appointee is not 100 per cent qualified: the fact is, few people are! One purpose of the interview should be to find a candidate who has about two-thirds of what you want, rather than spending the interview with each candidate trying to sell you the idea that he/she is 100 per cent qualified.

- The meetings with the worker should be quite frequent in the early stages, and not too formal. The objective is for the worker to get to know the job and the people involved—which means you too!

If these meetings are helpful and provide guidance the worker will soon feel wanted and supported and will become confident in the post. Then the meetings will not need to be so frequent. This will mean that a line of trusting communication has been formed which will enable the worker or the management group to grasp the nettle quickly if problems arise.

Running meetings—the agony and not much ecstasy

Despite the reams of paper and some excellent films on how to run meetings, the number I attend that are a pleasure to be at is very limited. They cannot all be fun, but they could be a lot less time-wasting and not leave you feeling that you would have been better employed doing something else.

Running a meeting, as chairperson, is a skilled business, but so is taking part in such a way as to be constructive, especially if the one in the chair is not very skilled. Improving one's ability requires development in three areas—*knowledge, attitudes* and *skills*. Knowledge and attitudes can be modified through reading or watching good practice, skills have to be practised against some measure of effectiveness and change in performance.

All I hope to do here is to relate a few of the more common behaviours and practices which have proved helpful in making for more efficient and effective meetings, both for chairs and participants. Once you know these, you can try them out and acquire greater skills through trial and error.

Chairing

Some of the more common complaints about chairs are:

- bias towards or against particular courses of action or people;
- lack of control in the meeting; too many talking at once, a few people dominating the meeting, others saying nothing, too much butting in or talking through others, too much repetition;
- lack of clear understanding of what was agreed;
- decisions not carried out.

When I look at writing and training materials on running meetings (including some of my own from the 1960s), I notice that a lot of it follows the 'shouldist' philosophy: 'The chairman *should* be unbiased, *should* have control, and *should* have done his preparation', etc. People may sometimes improve through exhortation, but having some definite guide-lines is generally more helpful than being told what we ought to be doing, which we usually know anyway!

In the chair—the hot seat

It is quite difficult to remain unbiased if you are in the chair when a matter is being discussed for which you favour a particular decision or course of action, especially if it involves your own work. If you try to influence the result you may be seen as biased and manipulative; if you give no opinion people may think you are devious, and be suspicious. Either way you lose. But don't despair, there are ways to overcome this:

(a) You can delegate the chair to someone else while a particular subject on which you want co-operation is under discussion. In this way you can express your arguments without having to think about running the meeting fairly at the same time.

(b) If, for some reason, it would not be realistic to give up the chair as suggested, you can delegate certain functions during the discussion, e.g. specific people can be asked;

- to watch out for and clarify any ambiguity or misunderstanding by either side, e.g. 'Tom, when you said "the balance of funds", did you mean the balance left out of the budget for that job, or the entire balance for maintenance for the year?'

- to summarise the main arguments and help people know where the meeting has got to. This can be done before a vote is taken, or after discussion if no vote is to be taken. It can also be done at an interim stage when people are feeling bogged down.

(c) There are proven behaviours used by effective chairs which enable them to be *seen* to be fair.* These are:

- *Proposals.* Concentrate on proposals to do with the *procedure* of the meeting rather than the subject matter, e.g. 'I suggest we discuss the fourth item on the agenda first, since time is short and Dave has to leave', or, 'We've been good at finding reasons *not* to do this, what about possible benefits?' You can often get your own subject proposal through by linking it with or building it on to someone else's.

- *Support or disagreement.* It is a good idea not to disagree on subject proposals brought up, but to support *people* rather than *issues*—'Thank you for raising this, George, what do others think?'

- *Clarifying.* Over 25 per cent of all your behaviour will be directed towards ensuring that people have the same understanding of what is going on as explained in (b) above.

---

*See Morgan and Rackham, *Inter-active Skills Training*, McGraw-Hill, 1976.

- *Asking questions.* This is a way of directing discussion along certain lines, exploring issues, and showing interest and involvement but appearing neutral at the same time. Nearly 30 per cent of a skilled chair's behaviour is spent on this (twice that of other group members'), whereas they spend much less time on

- *Giving information (especially opinions).* Concentrate more on facts which have to be made known by the person in the chair.

- *Non-verbal Behaviour.* It is known that when a subject being discussed is controversial or loaded, the chair looks at the speaker less than half the time the speaker is talking. When that speaker has finished the chair is likely to influence who speaks next. However, when the subject is fairly neutral, the chair looks at the speaker nearly three-quarters of the time, and seldom tries to influence who speaks next.

(d) *Control.* The way you keep control will vary according to the numbers present. In a small meeting of say 4–8 people, there is usually (though not always) more self-control than in larger meetings where the role of the chair is crucial. The larger the meeting, the more important the *clarifying* behaviour becomes.

Most of us do not realise how poor we are at listening. We see ourselves talking over the top of others less frequently than is actually the case; we see others doing it more (although people who do it a lot don't seem to notice when others do it to them!). If you tell people directly that they are interrupting or have spoken too often, they think you are biased, but you can do it more subtly. 'Not you George, you've already spoken on the subject' sounds more biased than, 'Hang on everybody, can we hear from those who haven't said anything yet? I'd like to get as many views as we can.'

Watch out too for people who, when things are going against them, quietly ask one or two neighbours a question, to distract them from the speaker's arguments. If this happens, it is time to clamp down, and stop the main speaker, saying, 'Can we all hear the point being made over in this corner?'. The main speaker can continue when there is silence.

(e) *Participation—large meetings.* Very often, for many people present, the chance to give their opinion to whoever will listen to it is more important than the outcome of the discussion. In a large meeting this can make things drag on if they can only say their bit to the whole meeting. A useful strategy in situations where there is a lot of interest is to introduce the subject and the objective of the meeting, and then to suggest that people spend a few minutes working out the main issues by discussion with those nearest to them. After letting people 'buzz' for a few minutes, call the meeting to order and suggest people keep to the main points.

(f) *Keeping to the point.* This can be one of the more frustrating problems. The chair can be trapped between not wanting to be rude, but needing to move the proceedings forward. There are a number of strategies you can adopt when people are not keeping to the point, but first of all you have to make the boundaries clear: for example, 'I think it will save time if we concentrate tonight on whether we should go ahead with the extension, and leave aside other questions such as who will put it up or how the bookings will be handled.'

Other strategies are:

- Stopping speakers who try to cover several points in one speech, e.g. 'I think that's a good point you've made over the budget, can we leave questions about the audit for now?'

- For speakers who have made several points you can summarise, picking out the points relevant to the discussion.

- Referring irrelevant comments to be brought up later if appropriate.

- 'Can we finish with Hazel's point about opening hours first, before we go on to what we sell?'

- People who ramble on too long and lose everyone can be reminded they have done so by asking them at the end of their spiel, 'I'm a bit lost, would you mind summarising the main points you made?'

152

- When people are not listening, but arguing repetitively, a useful strategy is to say, 'We have aired this pretty well, does anyone have anything to add which has not been said already?' This may give a chance to a quiet member who has been waiting, but more likely it means no further discussion since people realise that, not having listened, they cannot remember what has been said already!

Cool it

Once tempers get heated it can be quite tough work cooling them down again. The following are tried and tested means of reducing friction before it starts, or cooling the principal protagonists once they are locked in combat.

1. *Danger signals*
   A sure sign of tension and potential uproar is when people start using *irritating phrases*. These include such gems as:

   'With all *due respect*' (a sure signal a fast ball is being delivered!);
   'We've been very *fair* and *reasonable*' (by implication *you* are unreasonable);
   'Carry on *if you must*, if you've something *sensible* to say', (that'll make a change);
   '*At last*, we've *finally* got the figures', (any fool could have done them in half the time).

   All the words in italics add nothing to the development of an argument, nor to resolving an issue. All they do is to irritate or upset other people, especially those at whom they are directed, and they usually precede a set of emotionally charged exchanges.

   Counter action
   To counter these the chair can:

   - invite someone who has not yet spoken to give an opinion, to help out those who could be involved in a slanging match.
   - prevent those involved from speaking to each other directly, by asking them to explain to you directly what their problem is.

- give a summary of the alternatives open to those present.

2. *A one-to-one slanging match*
It is quite common for two people to get so worked up they cannot hear what the other is saying—even when other people can see that they are álmost in agreement!

Counter action
Instead of just remonstrating with the antagonists, set a ground rule that before putting any more arguments, each must summarise accurately what the other person is saying! It takes courage from the chair to insist, but it shows other people that you are in charge, *and* shows the two or three concerned how little they have listened.

3. *Bedlam*
Occasionally, a meeting may become completely chaotic with everyone talking at once, no one listening, and a few shouting.

Counter action
Suggest a five-minute break for informal discussion, and if possible a cup of tea. When people return to their chairs remind them of normal courtesies, such as one at a time, and warn that you will impose (2) above if necessary.

Being a Participant

As a member not in the chair you can often assist the process of the meeting by using some of the techniques given above. For example:

- You can take up genuine ambiguities and clarify them: 'Does the speaker mean . . ?'

- You can give a summary of where you think the meeting has got to, or ask the chair for one: 'Chair, I'm a bit confused. Where have we got to in this discussion?'

- You can encourage quieter members to speak: 'I'd like to hear from those who haven't spoken at all yet.'

- You can ensure all sides of a question are considered: 'We all seem to be in favour of this so far. Are there any snags we haven't thought of?'

- You can suggest to the chair before a meeting, that as he/she is known to hold strong views on one item on the agenda, he/she may be seen to be more impartial (and so be more successful), if someone else takes the chair during that item on the agenda.

- If you have an item for 'Any other business', tell the chair at the start, not at the end.

And finally—'We don't get on very well'

It is a very British trait, that when people disagree over priorities, or who should be doing what, or how decisions are made, or if someone has not told them something, to assume that it is a personal attack, and to respond in similar manner.

In fact the majority of issues which cause people not to get along with one another are not personality problems at all, they are only symptoms of one of the issues mentioned in this chapter. Once they are cleared up, the personal relationships involved also improve.

So it makes little sense to try to raise morale simply by tackling social interactions and ignoring the problems in the organisation. Otherwise, Saturday night's barbecue may be a great success, but once back at the old frustrations on Monday morning, all the goodwill from Saturday flies out of the window.

The National Youth Bureau has a useful set of materials on management committees, running meetings, and procedures; also a simulation exercise. Details from:

Young Volunteer Resources Unit,
National Youth Bureau,
17–23 Albion Street,
Leicester LE1 6GD

Paper work

Agendas and minutes are important. In some cases, e.g. if you make your project a limited company, they are a legal necessity. But very often they are much longer than necessary, or too ambiguous to be helpful.

Agendas: time can be saved if a brief background note is included rather than just the subject heading, e.g.:

- *Item 5. Holidays.* The field worker has asked to take three days of her annual holiday to follow on from the public holiday on April 21/22.

  It can also help if people know who is going to speak on an item, e.g.:

- *Item 10. Expansion.* Dave will outline a scheme for making shoes from old pine cones.

Don't let people sit thinking up 'any other business'. Ask if there is anything not on the agenda to be discussed at the *start*.

Minutes, on the other hand, are invariably too long and cumbersome, e.g.:

- *Item 5. Meeting with council officials.* Mary said that she thought it would not be necessary for everybody to attend the meeting, only those who were actually involved in the dispute with the Council at the start. Peter said that he thought that everyone who had any papers or views on the subject could pass them to those attending to help them in the discussion.

The chairperson and secretary need to think about the minutes and ask themselves:

- *Do those who receive them really need to know all the details of what was said, or just what conclusions were reached?'*

So the minutes above would read:

Item 5. Meeting with council officials.
- Only those involved in the dispute need attend.
- Anyone with papers or views to pass them on to Dave, Pete, John or Ros.

- *Do the minutes make clear who is to take the action agreed or follow up?*
  A right-hand column with the heading *Action by* ensures that people receiving the minutes can easily pick out who is responsible, e.g.:

Item 6. Publicity

Agreed   *Action by*

To draw up a new statement showing the   Ruth
aims, objectives and actions of the Centre,   Alison
aimed at organisations who might help with   Tony
funding.

Working It All Out

The foregoing is not intended to be comprehensive. There are a number of good 'Do It Yourself' management tools, some of which I have listed, which can provide further ideas on tackling the problems.

Sometimes it can help to use an outsider as a consultant. This need not be expensive. If you have a local polytechnic with business or management studies departments, staff or students will often be prepared to help in return for using the experience in their research or studies, possibly needing just expenses. Sometimes a donor can be found to fund someone to help.

Choosing a Consultant

If you hope to use a consultant, don't commit yourself to anyone just because he offers himself and will not cost much, or will be subsidised by someone else.

A few ways of finding out if a consultant will be a suitable 'fit' with your organisation are as follows:

- Get the would-be consultant to meet some of the people from your group. Try to find out his or her style of operating. If your problems are those of structures or administrative systems, you may prefer someone who is prescriptive. My personal preference, based on professional experience, is that regardless of the type of problem, it is more effective to have someone who will bring the 'clients' (i.e. you) themselves to solve their own problems. Prescribed solutions tend to be put on one side and not acted upon. The process by which clients are helped to solve their own problems is, or

157

should be, an educational one in which they learn lessons which stay with them.

- The consultant is a person, and like everyone else will have his or her own personality which may not feel comfortable with the clients'. In a preliminary discussion you should be able to see any difficulties *before* there is any commitment on either side.

- It is quite common and legitimate to ask consultants what sort of experience they have had, which other organisations they have worked with, and how they would approach the problems. What is also very revealing, or can be, is to ask for experiences which they felt were failures. A consultant who cannot tell you of a failure or two, or does not believe he *has* had any, has not learnt very much.

Mirroring the Community

If you are working as a group of people from a community with day to day contact in that community, you can obtain a very good idea of the fears, anxieties, hopes, conflicts, and issues important to people in that community, by examining those between and within members of your group. In other words, the group is a mirror of the wider community.

If you have the skills yourself to tease out and examine these feelings and issues, it can be very rewarding and give some real insights as to what is happening outside. But the mirror is not always crystal clear; sometimes you need a third party to help you look into it, and to take soundings from people before they begin discussing it with each other.

And finally—enjoy it!

If you are getting neither pleasure nor profit from all your exertions, why do it? The pleasure may be long-term satisfaction rather than short-term hysteria; the profit may be in what you learn rather than cash in the bank. If there is no prospect of either and your whole project is weighing you down—cut your losses and run.

But hopefully you will have fun *and* learn something. My experience of self-help activities is that they are much better learning places than any academic management course, and can help us gain skills and confidence. Working with other people gives us new knowledge in many areas, and enriches each individual in a whole variety of ways. Traditional academic means cannot replace personal experience. Learning from the type of experience I have described in this book comes from the exchange of feelings and emotions, and the rejection of a belief in the infallibility of existing systems or experts, from searching for and trying out alternatives, from a commitment to relationships and involvement, and from holding values and beliefs as important as facts.

If we accept this for ourselves and help those we are involved with to experience it in the same way, we may help them achieve far more than the immediate or more obvious goals we have worked out in our project or self-help activity. We should also be able to work up a sense of excitement and challenge which will keep other people committed and involved.